BEYOND THE EDGE

Freedom to Journey into the Unknown

Joseph W. Holloway, PhD

WestBow Press books may be ordered through booksellers or by contacting:

WestBow Press
A Division of Thomas Nelson
1663 Liberty Drive
Bloomington, IN 47403
www.westbowpress.com
1-(866) 928-1240

ISBN: 978-1-4497-8139-2 (sc)

Library of Congress Control Number: 2013900386

Printed in the United States of America

WestBow Press rev. date: 02/05/2013

For my wife Debby and my sister Sue.

TABLE OF CONTENTS

Prologue ix

Introduction xv

Part 1

The Death Tax: Ruled by the Edge........ 1

Chapter 1 Dealing with Mortality: A Fixation on the Edge 3

Chapter 2 The Covenant with Death: The Edge Effect 22

Part 2

The Repeal of the Death Tax: Ruling the Edge 51

Chapter 3 Breaking the Covenant with Death:
Looking Beyond the Edge 53

Chapter 4 The Covenant with Life: Taking the Edge Off 80

Chapter 5 Pioneer Living: On Both Sides of the Edge 99

Epilogue 129

PROLOGUE

Cowboy Up. My heroes have always been cowboys. I gained the appreciation for cowboys when I was a wee lad growing up on a west Texas cattle farm. The seeds for my appreciation may have been planted by my mother who often read to me my favorite book *Brave Cowboy Bill*.[1] By the term cowboy, I am not referring to the modern variety that rides mechanical bulls in bars. The heroic character I envision is the romantic type that was attracted to the American frontier during the latter half of the 19th century; he is only incidentally a cowboy. The qualifications that make him heroic are not necessarily related to the ability to round up or work cows. Rather, these "cowboy" qualifications could be associated with the toughness required not only to survive, but to thrive under the stringent conditions afforded by life on the frontier. He is more than a *Survivor* as depicted in the current TV show; he survives in order to accomplish something; he is going somewhere. He is a journeyman, a pioneer, a frontiersman, willing to risk life and limb for the well-being of the wagon train or for the safety of his compadres as he traverses the frontier, the edge of civilization.

The Pioneers. The character that I admire and believe many would like to emulate is captured by C.M. Russell in his painting *The Wagon Boss*. The wagon boss exudes independence, confidence and competence. He

1 *Brave Cowboy Bill*, Kathryn and Byron Jackson, Richard Scarry, Illustrator, Little Golden Book #93 1st A ed. 1950, Simon and Schuster, NY.

knows the hazards of the trail and is prepared to handle them. He knows where he is going and he knows how to get there. He is brave and bold, having certain knowledge that he will overcome any and all obstacles. This idealized frontiersman is the embodiment of freedom. He travels light and is unencumbered; he is not burdened with bulky gear. Nor is he weighed down with psychological baggage such as doubt, fear or guilt. This kind of hero has a certain presence about him that demands respect and engenders confidence. One knows instinctively not to mess with him. He is ready to tackle any challenge that might arise on the frontier.

The Edge. The frontier is the edge of knowledge and security beyond which the law has no jurisdiction. We are fascinated with the idea of the frontier. As Fredrick Jackson Turner famously said "We don't have to live on the frontier (on the Edge) to be controlled by it."[2] Prudence dictates that frontiersmen acquire professional help as they travel into the unknown. Since the human race has generally been, and still is, on the move, physical frontiers have always existed and the pioneer type has always been idolized. The preponderance of archeological and genetic evidence indicates that humanity has been migrating across the face of the globe for millennia, even prior to historic documentation. Apparently, the urge to be on the move and the lure of the frontier is in the very fabric of our being. Thus, it is likely that this pioneer type has been idolized long before recorded history. In our personal journeys through life, we each face a series of frontiers, of boundaries or edges, but the most domineering edge of all is the Edge of life; we call this Edge, death. Because each of us is on this personal journey guarded by the edges of birth and death, we each need this kind of hero/leader. What's more, we want to become this kind of hero.

Cowboy College. If this heroic type is so attractive, the question is, how can we acquire his character traits? Underlying questions include: What does he have that others lack? What do we need to do to become this

---

2 *The Significance of the Frontier in American History,* 1893, Frederick Jackson Turner.

kind of hero ourselves? Or more to the point, what flaw do we possess that prevents us from living as the heroic pioneer not intimidated by the Edge? The answers to these questions are presented in fullness by the most authoritative authors to have ever lived: Moses, Isaiah, Paul, and John. Their writings are preserved for all time in the Bible and are the bases for this book.

Illusions. According to Isaiah 28, our tragic flaw is that we are encumbered with a wrong mindset that prevents us from being all we can be. That mindset is embodied in the seemingly innocuous adage, "eat, drink and be merry for tomorrow you may die".[3] That wrong mindset originates from our narrow perspective as humans. Our perspective is narrow because of our limitations. We are limited in both time and space by our mortal condition as ruled by the edges. From this narrow perspective it seems obvious that our primary problem as humans is that we have only a short time to live. This might be tolerable except for the fact that this realization occurs to us early in life. So, early on, we inevitably fall into the self-confining trap of letting the time we have to live be ruled by our knowledge of the shortness of our time. Isaiah called this mindset our "Covenant with Death".

Witness Protection. We are (at least subliminally) frightened by the impending doom of the ever-present specter of death. We expend considerable effort to ameliorate this fear including plunging the fear into our sub-consciousness. Through this effort, we build "safe houses" for ourselves. These "safe houses" then inadvertently serve as prisons that limit both our ability and our willingness to take risks. We voluntarily check ourselves into these prisons as a part of our "witness protection

3 Isaiah 22 "13 And behold joy and gladness, slaying oxen, and killing sheep, eating flesh, and drinking wine: let us eat and drink; for to morrow we shall die. 14 And it was revealed in mine ears by the LORD of hosts, Surely this iniquity shall not be purged from you till ye die, saith the Lord GOD of hosts." KJV. It is ironic that we remember the adage like it was an exhortation, when actually, the Lord condemned this line of thought and the actions stemming from it.

program"[4], but the constraints they induce are real just the same. We are occupied with our mortality to the extent that we tether ourselves to our self-built confines, further compounding our inherent limitations. Because of this self-imposed imprisonment, we fail to live boldly and confidently. We are afraid of the frontier. As we live in fear, we increasingly limit our range of action. Our purpose in doing this is to protect ourselves from the object of our fear: the frontier itself. Instead, we shackle ourselves with limitations that can be viewed as taxes we voluntarily charge ourselves. These taxes impede us and prevent us from experiencing true freedom. But, since these taxes are tolls we charge ourselves, we are not put out by paying them, and therefore underestimate the toll they take on us, their true cost.

The Scout Master. Paul alludes to Isaiah 28 in Romans 9:33-10:11where he draws the conclusion that there is only one way for us to rid ourselves of these self-imposed shackles. We must develop confidence in the only true pioneer, Jesus Christ. Paul explains that Jesus is the only true pioneer because He is the only one to have pioneered the frontier of death, exploring both sides of the grave. He alone has the means to help us in our plight against death. Contrary to Gene Roddenberry's lead-in to *Star Trek,* space is not the final frontier; death is. Moses tells us in Numbers 10 that we can boldly go into the unknown if we follow the lead of the servant of the covenant as symbolized by the Ark of the Covenant. In John 14, Jesus alludes to Numbers 10 when He tells His disciples that the pioneering way is the way of confidence - confidence in Himself as the true servant of the covenant.

Real Living. The intent of this book is to show how these scriptures reveal the way to drop the self-imposed taxes that fetter us, thereby freeing us to pioneer living. Because the "Covenant with Death" and the resultant "Death Tax" are not broadly understood concepts, much

4 We witness death all our lives. The first formal witness protection program in the United States was provided by the Ku Klux Klan Act in 1871. http://en.wikipedia.org

of this book (Part 1) is about our obsession with mortality. As you read this book, it is important to remember the statement of one of the greatest cowboys/pioneers who never lived, Augustus McRae in Larry McMurtry's *Lonesome Dove*.[5] His statement fits this writing: "It's not dying I'm talking about..., it's living".

5 *Lonesome Dove*, 1982, Larry McMurtry, ISBN 067001167/0-671-00116-7. The protagonist Augustus McRae, although fictitious, was patterned after Oliver Loving while his compadre, Woodrow Call was patterned after Charles Goodnight, historical cattlemen of the plains of Texas.

INTRODUCTION

The Old, Old Story. This book has two concurrent but related themes: it is both a story book and a mystery book. The story involves the basic issue of our lives: our mortality problem. It addresses a series of sub-issues: the method that seems appropriate for fixing the problem, the flaw inherent in this method, the ramifications of the flawed fix on the quality of our lives (the death tax), the only avenue of escape from our flawed fix, and the freedom we gain from this escape that allows us to live as pioneers overcoming the intimidation inflicted by the Edge. The mystery involves the method by which this story is revealed to us. The Biblical scriptures were, for the most part, not written to be mysteries, but many have become mysterious as a natural result of their background. First, they were written over a long period of time in long-forgotten historical contexts and cultures that we cannot now experience intimately. Second, they were written in Hebrew, Aramaic, and Greek. Not only do we not understand these languages but some of the words have meanings that have changed over time as the cultural and historical contexts changed. Third, although each Hebrew and Greek word had meaning, many of the words cannot now be translated into English succinctly, and English has no verb forms that correspond to some of those used in the original tongues. Fourth, scripture was originally written in a non-punctuated, run-on form so that we must now guess at the punctuation and at topic differentiation.

Fifth, the scriptures have been studied intensively over long periods of time and some have been endowed with meanings not intended by the original authors. These endowments have become baggage that has become an almost impenetrable barrier to understanding their original meanings.

The Illusive Allusion. A sixth reason the Bible has become mysterious to us is that the scriptures are products of the work of scribes who recorded oral traditions and stories that had been handed down by word of mouth for indeterminate periods of time. Thus the scriptures that we read today have had input by an unknown number of people and their input is composited into the scripture. A seventh related reason is the teaching style of the oral tradition. Much of the New Testament writing was an accumulation of reports of oral teachings that were performed in the form of the style practiced by the western Diaspora rabbis of the time, the *remez* (Hebrew for hint or allusion).[6] In this form of teaching, rabbis took for granted the extensive memories of learned pupils. Because of this, they were able to use short, integral segments or "code words" taken from Old Testament passages that brought to the minds of the students, detailed memories of the larger contexts. Through linking together these code words, rabbis were able to make new points or elaborate on old themes succinctly. Difficulty in understanding these *remez'* is often compounded by the fact that these rabbis (including Jesus) did not primarily quote from the original Old Testament Hebrew or Aramaic, but from an intermediary Greek translation called the Septuagint. This document was the result of the work of seventy (seventy-two?) scholars amassed in Alexandria, Egypt by Ptolemy II Philadelphus in the third century BCE. This translation was understood intimately by many Jews in the first century AD.[7] The

6 *Exploring Bible Times: The Gospels in Context*, 2007, James C. Martin, Bible World Seminars, Amarillo, TX, Preserving Bible Times.

7 *The Septuagint with Apocrypha: Greek and English*, 1851, Sir Lancelot C.L.Brenton, Samuel Bagster & Sons, Ltd, London.

modern reader of these New Testament passages is not familiar with this document and does not have the background or comprehensive memories of the original pupils. Therefore, modern students do not recognize the code words used in the *remez'* and thus do not make the leap to the concepts explained in the longer passages to which the *remez'* allude.

Common Sense. The culmination of these seven characteristics of the Bible is that we have lost the richness and vitality of many Biblical themes that are important to us. The ancient understanding of the impact of our Covenant with Death on our lives is therefore a mystery to us. We fail to see that the Bible, although written by many people over a long period of time, is one comprehensive, unerring story told in several concurrently developed, fundamental, interrelating themes. These themes include: the nature of good and evil as related to death, the search for ways to overcome the inherent futility of living, the necessity of confidence in God for successful living, the relationship of sacrifice and rightness, the relative effectiveness of negative and positive motivation, the benevolence of God toward man, the intrinsic contradictory duality (or trinity) in the nature of God as it relates to the role of man's free will in determining his future, and the overwhelming force of death as it affects the quality of life. This latter theme, which is embedded in the other themes, is the subject of this book. These interrelating themes are each rooted in both the character of man and the character of God. Thus, they connect the pithiness of man to the intangibleness of God. As a result, each of these themes resonates deeply within us, often striking unexpected chords that reverberate throughout our being. These deeply ingrained themes are integral parts of the fabric of our being whether we recognize it or not. As we explore this theme (the necessity for all of us to deal with the fact of our earthly mortality), we will gain insight into who we are, why we are limited in meeting success, and how we can rise above it all. Many parts of the Bible amplify this theme, too many to be included in this book. Therefore, this book is limited to a central set of select scriptures, those required for an understanding of this theme. This central set will provide a foundation to understand other scriptures related to this theme. Unfortunately, our failure to grasp the transcendental issues of the Bible has led to this theme being overlooked as being a central driver of our lives.

Laying it Out. This book will both tell the story of our struggle with our mortality and reveal the mystery of how the Bible divulges this story. The format is the narrative of the overarching story in the text[8] with the supporting exposition of the scripture presented in foot notes. This allows the reader to read only the text if the goal is to understand the story. However, the footnotes are provided to give the basis for the story, the supporting evidence of how the story came into being. This supporting documentation is made by analyzing each *remez* in context, presenting the scriptures by subtopic in the order written and as translated in the King James Version. The footnotes are arranged

8 *Commentary on the Old Testament,* 1996, Kiel, C.F. and F. Delitzsch, Hendrickson Publishers, Inc., Peabody, MA, ISBN 13-97809-135-73884;*The Interlinear Hebrew-Aramaic Old Testament Volumes I and III,* 1976, Jay P. Green, Sr., Hendrickson Publishers, Peabody, MA, ISBN 0913-573-30-2; *The Interlinear Greek-English New Testament Volume IV,* 1976, Jay P. Green, Sr., Hendrickson Publishers, Peabody, MA, ISBN 0913-573-30-2; *The Expositor's Greek Testament, Volume II, St. Paul's Epistle to the Romans,* 1988, James Denney, W. Robertson Nicoll, Ed., Wm. B. Eerdmans Publishing Co., Grand Rapids, MI, ISBN 0-8028-2108-1; *The Expositor's Greek Testament Volume I,1I, The Gospel of St. John,* 1988, Marcus Dods, W. Robertson Nicoll, Ed., Wm. B. Eerdmans Publishing Co., Grand Rapids, MI, ISBN 0-8028-2108-1; *Interlinear Transliterated Bible,* Copyright © 1994, 2003 by Biblesoft, Inc.; *Novum Testamentum Graece Nestle-Aland 27th Ed.* © 1898 and 1993 by Deutsche Bibelgesellschaft, Stuttgart; *PCSB Greek and PCSB Hebrew fonts,* Copyright © 1992, Galaxie Software, Garland, TX; *Interlinear Transliterated Bible,* Copyright © 1994, 2003 by Biblesoft, Inc.; *Novum Testamentum Graece Nestle-Aland 27th Ed.* © 1898 and 1993 by Deutsche Bibelgesellschaft, Stuttgart; *PCSB Greek and PCSB Hebrew fonts,* Copyright © 1992, Galaxie Software, Garland, TX; *Old Testament: Biblia Hebraica Stuttgartensia,* Copyright © 1967/77, 1983, Deutsche Bibelgesellschaft Stuttgart.

so that the word definitions[9] most pertinent to the text are bolded and italicized so that they may be read as a continuous text across footnotes in an "author's amplified version" of the scripture. I begin my discussion with the scripture that initially served as the key to unlock the door by which I entered into the domain encompassing the ramifications of our Covenant with Death. This scripture is Paul's *remez* on the Covenant in Romans 9:33-10:11. This *remez* is an allusion to Isaiah 28 which is the point of entry into a major perspective on the meaning of salvation. Paul's prelude to his *remez* in the first part of Romans is a picture of life as a journey. Jesus amplifies the most important dimension to that imagery through his own *remez* recorded in John 14: 1-4. His *remez* builds on the *Torah* in Numbers 10:29-36. This book will expose these two *remez'* as they reveal the natural basis for our Covenant with Death, our ability to hide the Covenant from ourselves, the ramifications of this Covenant on our lives in terms of the inherent self-imposed death tax, the only real avenue for escape from paying the death tax, and the true nature of our life's journey. Death is inevitable, but the perpetuation of the death tax is not. We don't have

---

9 *The New Strong's Exhaustive Concordance of the Bible*, 1990, Thomas Nelson Publishers, Nashville, TN, ISBN 0-8407-6750-1; *Word Pictures of the New Testament*, 1933, A.T. Robertson, Baker Book House, Grand Rapids, MI, ISBN 0-8010-7710-9; *A Comprehensive Dictionary of the Original Greek Words with their Precise Meanings for English Readers*, 1947, W.E. Vine, MacDonald, McLean, VA, ISBN 0-917006-03-8; *The Complete Word Study New Testament with Parallel Greek*, 1992, Spiros Zodhiates, AMG Intl., Chattanooga, TN, ISBN 0 89957-652-4; *The Complete Word Study Old Testament*, Spiros Zodhiates, 1994, AMG Intl., Chattanooga, TN, ISBN 0-89957-665-6; *Thayer's Greek-English Lexicon of the New Testament*, 4th Edition, 1901, Joseph Henry Th ayer, Baker Book House, Grand Rapids, MI, ISBN 0-8010-8838-0; *Word Pictures in the New Testament, Volume IV, The Epistles of Paul*, 1931, Archibald Thomas Robertson Baker Book House, Grand Rapids MI, ISBN 0-8010-7710-9; *The New Brown, Driver, Briggs, Gesenius Hebrew and English Lexicon*, 1979, Francis Brown, S.R. Driver, Charles A. Briggs, Hendrickson Publishers, Peabody, MA, ISBN 0-913573-20-5; *Wuest's Word Studies From the Greek New Testament for the English Reader, Volume I*, 1955, Wm. B. Eerdmans Publishing Co., Grand Rapids, MI, ISBN 0-8028-2280-0.

to pay it all of our lives. An extraordinary event was required to inform us of our only opportunity to escape death tax payment. That event can revolutionize our thinking about our mortality and free us to live the pioneering life on both sides of the Edge tax free.

PART 1

The Death Tax: Ruled by the Edge

"She should have died hereafter;
There would have been a time for such a word.
To-morrow, and to-morrow, and to-morrow,
Creeps in this petty pace from day to day
To the last syllable of recorded time,
And all our yesterdays have lighted fools
The way to dusty death. Out, out, brief candle!
Life's but a walking shadow, a poor player
That struts and frets his hour upon the stage
And then is heard no more: it is a tale
Told by an idiot, full of sound and fury,
Signifying nothing."

Macbeth, V.v., 1605, William Shakespeare.

CHAPTER 1

DEALING WITH MORTALITY: A FIXATION ON THE EDGE

"You can check-out any time you like,
But you can never leave!'"

The Hotel California, 1976, Joe Walsh, Glenn Frey, Don Henley, 1976, Eagles, album *Hotel California*.

Contexts: Moons and Junes and Ferris Wheels.[10] Only a few events are universally experienced by all people, no matter when and where they live. Some of us have been thrilled by the loss of our stomachs when we are dropped out of the sky by a roller coaster at the state fair. Many of us have savored the juicy fruitiness of a fresh peach. Most of us have been inspired by the rising of a harvest moon on a crisp autumn evening. Whatever experiences we may have in common, only two are universally experienced by all people who have ever lived: each of us is born and each of us dies. Because of these two universal experiences, all humanity feels a kindred spirit and communion. We all live on the Edge. Although, for the most part, we are born and die separately, because of the ever-present

10 "I've looked at life from both sides now, From up and down and still somehow, It's life's illusions I recall, I really don't know life at all." From *Both Sides Now*, 1969, written and sung by Joni Mitchell, album Clouds.

consciousness of our common trauma in birth and impending death, we feel we are all in this thing together. We each, regardless of how long we might live, must deal with one common issue, the personal problem of mortality. As far as we know, *Homo sapiens* is the only specie that is mortal, has foreknowledge of that mortality, and alters the course of life according to this knowledge. In fact the knowledge of our certain death hangs over us like a black cloud all the days of our lives.

The Well-Trodden Way: the Roads of Death.[11] According to Proverbs 14:12, "There is a way which seemeth right unto a man, but the end thereof are the ways of death." On the face of it, our manner of life comes to us in a natural way. We just take it as it comes to us. We are all born pretty much in the same way; we all have the same needs; we all learn to cry early in life when things go against us. The course of life seems to flow naturally to us. There is only one problem. This course is guided by the obvious fact that we will die like every man who has ever lived. Our life is therefore governed by this "fact". But, what if there is more to us than our physical being? What if this other part doesn't necessarily "pass away"? What if this other part of us is the main part, our essence? If these implications are true, does this change the way we live?

The Certainty of Death and Taxes.[12] Our struggle with the problem of mortality is embedded in our daily existence encumbering us in at least twelve ways. In the following paragraphs I will discuss these sometimes innovative means we use to attenuate this problem. The "by-product" of

---

11 Proverbs 14:12 "There is a way", *yeesh derek*, ***there stands out a road as the obvious way to live...*** [from *dawrak'* = to tread, manner, journey], "which seemeth right unto a man", *yaashaar*, ***that is convenient***, straight, pleasant, prosperous [from *yawshar'* = causing pleasantness, prosperity], *lipneey-iysh*, ***on the face of it to mortal man***, the extant one...[from pawneem' = face], "but the end thereof", *w^{a}achriytaah*, Wah conjunctive of*'achariyth* = ***in conjunction with*** [the way that stands out as the obvious way to go]..., ***what comes after...***[from akhar' = the hind part, that coming after], Septuagint has *teleutaia* = the goal of [the road] is,"are the ways of death", *daarkey*, ***are the roads***, journeys..., *maawet* = ***[governed by] death*** [as the destination of the journey].

12 *The Political History of the Devil*, 1726, Daniel Defoe.

this effort is the suffering we create for ourselves usually without knowing it. These self-inflicted wounds can be viewed as forms of "personal tax" that we voluntarily, if unwittingly, charge ourselves. First, we feel driven to make a difference with our lives. Second, we feel driven to have certain experiences while "we still can". Third, we believe we deserve to live the high life and feel deprived if expectations don't become reality. Fourth, we are impatient for the "highs" of life, and thus have a penchant for creating artificial highs by taking needless risks. Fifth, we judge the quality of our lives by the proportion of time we can classify as "good" providing opportunity for disgruntlement. Sixth, we are insatiably preoccupied with a search for Ponce de Leon's Fountain of Youth. Seventh, even love and romance, life's most personal, and potentially most satisfying experiences, are made possible only if the alternative is impending loss. Eighth, we are vulnerable to any tactic that holds out the possibility of eternalness. Ninth, we work hard to escape from the issue of our mortality. Tenth, our attempt to escape results in chronic stress, providing vulnerability for any additional stress to send us "over the top". Eleventh, given that we cannot escape, we become anxious about our fate. Twelfth, to compound our inability to escape, our anxiety can become chronic, leading to despondency. This book explores the Biblical bases of these forms of self-taxation. As a matter of introduction and overview, however, at the outset I will describe each form of tax as to its impact on our lives. Not everyone experiences every form of the tax to the same degree, but because we all must deal with our mortality, we all feel the brunt of some form of self-taxation. Collectively, humankind is insatiably and chronically absorbed in each expression of our issue with mortality.

The First Tax: Driven. Our occupation with transience, which results from our mortal condition, is expressed in terms of our drive to live lives that matter. We want to believe that our lives make a difference and that we do not live in vain. Because we are cognizant of the shortness of our time, we feel an urgency to drive ourselves to live meaningful lives. We have difficulty living up to expectations, whether the expectations originate from within us or from someone else. We drive ourselves to leave a legacy. A legacy is our attempt at gaining a facsimile of immortality. Almost from the time of our birth, we feel "under the gun" to accomplish. We feel guilty about wasting time or even about accomplishment if it is tardy because we know "the clock is ticking". We feel pressured to be different from our contemporaries who we perceive to live nonproductive, mundane lives. We want to "measure up" by accomplishing more than those who have gone before who we believe have left little mark on the earth. *Carpe diem* is the rule we live by: we are driven to seize the day. We are vulnerable to this rule regardless of our age or stage of life. We tell ourselves we will go beyond the ordinary. Our basic fear is that only two words will be engraved on our tombstones, those words being, "ho hum". When life unveils in a manner to indicate we are falling into the old, established, dull ruts of our ancestors or our colleagues, we try to escape from the vision of our personal mediocrity. If escape is not possible, in desperation, we attempt to "break out", pushing ourselves to meet standards that may only exist in our minds. This drive to be significant is expressed as we live in terms of urgency and futility, subtle but substantial currencies of the death tax. We urgently feel the need to live meaningful and exhilarating lives. Any perceived failure in this regard is felt as futility. Thus, we find it difficult to live gracious and graceful lives. Many people driven by their Covenant with Death are viewed by their peers as being successful. Their success is bought at a great expense, the "Driven" death tax. The expense takes a large toll on the taxpayer, but the success purchased is deemed to be "worth it" by the earthbound beneficiaries of the hard-earned products of the success. This is true mainly because the beneficiaries were not required to pay the tax themselves. Such was the case at Steven Jobs' death. Most people on the earth benefited from his success. A longer view of his relatively extreme case is that the resulting purchased success is temporary. Any invention, no matter how innovative, will ultimately be supplanted by other eclipsing inventions: witness Bill Lear's eight track tape, but death is permanent.[13] No one can be against success in attaining life's goal or argue that there is some urgency in achieving that success. The tax comes when achievement becomes obsession, when the take-home message is the "driven" part. One can argue that the success is not worth the tax.[14]

The Second Tax: The Bucket List[15] A possible view of this first tax is that it may have substantial influence on our lives, but we "get over it" once we "arrive". After we retire and accomplish our life's work, surely then the pressure is off and we can relax. Of course, many never reach that point. We either find that we never quite arrive, or even if we can trick ourselves into believing that we have arrived, we invent other hurdles to jump. If we can't accomplish these mind gymnastics, we must face the fact that life has become meaningless (no new frontiers to conquer). Many people

---

13 Many people who are "driven" also "drive" their children. In that way, this form of taxation (like death itself) becomes a highly heritable trait. In frustration from not being able to leave a satisfactory personal legacy, one can always gain some level of immortality by living through the children. Someone must carry on the family name in order to leave a real legacy and be "immortal". Worldwide, there is pressure to have male children to gain at least one generation of immortality "carrying on the family name". We are almost desperate to gain immortality one way or the other.

14 Ecclesiastes 1: "1 The words of the Preacher, the son of David, king in Jerusalem. 2 Vanity of vanities, saith the Preacher, vanity of vanities; all is vanity. 3 What profit hath a man of all his labour which he taketh under the sun? 4 One generation passeth away, and another generation cometh: but the earth abideth for ever. 5 The sun also ariseth, and the sun goeth down, and hasteth to his place where he arose. 6 The wind goeth toward the south, and turneth about unto the north; it whirleth about continually, and the wind returneth again according to his circuits. 7 All the rivers run into the sea; yet the sea is not full; unto the place from whence the rivers come, thither they return again. 8 All things are full of labour; man cannot utter it: the eye is not satisfied with seeing, nor the ear filled with hearing."

15 *The Bucket List*, 2007, film directed by Rob Reiner, written by Justin Zacham, starring Jack Nickolson and Morgan Fairchild. A telltale sign that we are controlled by a more sinister motive than our desire to make history is our inability to enjoy leisure time. We feel compelled to structure our vacations in a way to provide a guise of nobleness or accomplishment (e.g. hunting, fishing, educational cruises, *etc.*)

that fail to accomplish this mind trick soon die after retirement or other accomplishment because they "have nothing to live for". We, somehow, configure our lives to never attain the nirvana of contentment. So, a good sign of our willingness to pay this form of death tax throughout our lives is that even after we have arrived at a certain status (maybe even retire), we still can't give it up. We develop, maybe only unofficially, a list of things to be occupied with (or possibly a list of thrills we want to experience). We inadvertently admit that we are living out the payment of a death tax by calling this list our "Bucket List", thereby raising the status of these endeavors to that of a "job" we are driven to perform. The Bucket List amounts to the benchmarks set in our new "job description". Through this mechanism, we manage to continue to feel "under the gun" for however long we live.

The Third Tax: Living it Up. Because we are all fundamentally transient creatures and because (possibly not coincidentally) exhilarating events do not last, we inadvertently are reminded of our transience each time we experience exhilaration. Because each exhilarating event never lasts very long, the experience itself subliminally reminds us that our lives don't last very long either. Thus, even the most exhilarating experience can have a taint that is subtly unsettling. It seems unfair that the most exciting of times comes with a vague dread because, in the back of our minds, we know these times are fleeting just as life itself is fleeting. Growing up in west Texas, I had ample initiation into the unsettling feeling created by the highs of life. One particular experience stands out. A pernicious set of rumors communicated in whispered conversation during recess at Merkel High School, gelled over time into a legend. This legend involved the "adventures" of the High School freshman FFA dairy judging team at the district contest at the John Tarleton Agricultural College in Stephenville, 200 miles from Merkel. Freshman FFA members (aptly called Greenhand Farmers) considered that the 200 mile trip freed them to "pull out all stops" to create these adventures. The legend involved the various "historic" antics created by a sequence of teams over time who, in various ways, defied authority to create illicit high times. So, when it came to our time to contribute to this legend, we felt some pressure to deliver the best antic ever (or, at least have the best story to tell). So, my colleagues (the other four team members) wasted no time once we were left to our own resources after arriving in Stephenville. In the blistering afternoon sun, they walked to the nearest liquor store, exaggerated their age, and bought a case of the cheapest (hottest) beer in the store ironically named "Grand Prize". The name was ironic since we had been charged to win the Grand Prize at the contest not drink it. We cooled the foaming suds by running cold water over them in the bath tub of our motel room. After a "satisfactory" cool down period (about 30 minutes), there was competition in consumption. The high time (less than an hour) was accentuated immediately by the consequent contrasting low (a night of throwing up). By morning, neither the hotel room nor the Greenhands smelled very good. During our early-morning ride to the contest, my colleagues appeared "a bit green about the gills" and were forced to request that our FFA teacher, who was driving us, stop at a service station so they could "use the bathroom". During the contest, I noticed that my fellow team members mostly laid in the shade of a live oak tree, reflecting on the "high life" legacy they were establishing. Needless to say, the legacy did not include winning the Grand Prize. The experience has given me pause over time to reflect on the transiency of it all. This taxation is in the form of a subtle taint felt during exhilarating events that, by all rights, should result in pure pleasure.

The Fourth Tax: The Thrill of Victory, The Agony of Defeat.[16] It is unfortunate that excitement can only be experienced when contrasted to a backdrop deemed to be mundane or routine (or even catastrophic). This seems to be a "fixed law" since we are physiologically "hard-wired" so that during exhilaration we experience the euphoric psychological effects of endorphin (a morphine-like hormone) and epinephrine

16 "Spanning the globe to bring you the constant variety of sport… the thrill of victory… and the agony of defeat… the human drama of athletic competition… This is *ABC's Wide World of Sports!*", 1961-1998, Stanley Ralph Ross for *ABC's Wide World of Sports*.

surges to be followed by withdrawal symptoms when these hormones wane. The rareness and transience of the experience heightens the exhilaration by deepening the contrast with the mundane. So, it is physiologically impossible to attain our goal of extended and frequent intense exhilaration. It is ironic that if an exciting event is experienced frequently with duration and intensity, that event, over time, becomes mundane, losing its edge. We, however, have difficulty accepting this "fact of life". Because of the need to establish this contrast, extreme exhilaration is usually not possible unless the alternative is more severe than just being mundane. The thrilling high usually must be in contrast with a risk that is taken where the alternative is catastrophe. We are, therefore, willing to take inordinate risks to create the excitement we feel we deserve. We have taken this to the extremity of artificially creating these exhilarating "highs" through creating potential alternatives of "near death" experiences. Examples of this include surfing the killer waves off the shores of Hawaii, bungee jumping anywhere, mountain or rock wall climbing, and many other forms of "extreme sport", including nearly every event in the winter Olympics. Another approach at artificially creating these "highs" is through the use of alcohol, narcotics, or other stimulating drugs. We can also use illegitimacy to create "higher highs". Acts that otherwise would not be exhilarating can become so if performed illegitimately, thereby creating the contrasts necessary to define exhilaration. Some have transcended legal and moral boundaries to right the perceived injustices associated with, what seems to be, being forced to live a mundane life. They may take these risks as a part of the gambit required to achieve exhilaration. Thereby, they have put at risk any successes in life in hopes of enhancing life's excitement. This form of the tax impacts us through the physical and psychological bruising and breaking that we inflict upon ourselves in creating the necessary contrast in our gallant attempt to live an exhilarating life. We seem to live by the adage of "live free or die hard".[17]

---

17 *Live Free or Die Hard*, 2007, film directed by Len Wiseman and starring Bruce Willis.

The Fifth Tax: Monday Was Never Good Anyway.[18] A by-product of our desire to live exhilarating lives is that we partition our lives into "good" times and "bad" times. We judge the quality of our lives sometimes by the proportion of time we can classify as "good", or maybe we call these "quality times". We did not invent this way of thinking; many cultures have classified life in terms like these. For example, the Greek culture in the first century A.D. exhibited this human ability to classify time to the extent that they viewed time as two-dimensional: *chronos* was linear time measured quantitatively (chronology: the logos [word] about quantitative time); *kairos* was the value of time, the qualitative dimension (kairology; the word about the opportune time). When time attained a certain quality, certain events were possible and not one second before. For example, when *kairos* was right, a mare could come into heat and be receptive to a stallion regardless of the *chronos*. An example from the Bible is that "in due time" (*kairon*), "Christ died for the ungodly".[19] We think of our lives in this qualitative way. We look forward to certain exhilarating events, and wonder why they don't occur sooner or more frequently. Each of us believes we deserve the "highs" of life. We commonly bemoan the fact that the "highs" are few, fleeting and far between. Each of us has attempted to make the "highs" more frequent, more exciting, and of longer duration. We often feel cheated if the "highs" we experience lack intensity or don't occur frequently. In spite of the "facts of life" stated in the previous paragraph, we would like to believe that we can experience extended, intense excitement often. We find ourselves agreeing with Mrs. Muir in Forster's *A Passage to India* when she said, "Adventures do occur, but not punctually".[20] We sometimes say that "time weighs on us". If we dwell on the fact that we have to live through long periods of

---

18 *Except for Monday*, 1991, written by Reed Nielsen, recorded by Lorrie Morgan, album *Something in Red*.

19 Romans 5:6, "in due time Christ died for the ungodly", KJV: *Christos..eti kata kairon huper aseboon apothanen*.

20 *A Passage to India*, 1924, E.M. Forster, Harcort Brace Jovanovich, Inc., ISBN 0-89577-334-1.

"bad" times in order to experience the "good", this can produce a chronic dissatisfaction that undercuts our ability to enjoy time at all.

The Sixth Tax: Mirror, Mirror.[21] Our culture has a major distraction with the search for the means to stay young. If we are forced to face the inevitable fact that we cannot stay young, a fallback plan is to at least maintain the illusion of youth. Evidence of our preoccupation with our mortality is in the fact that we are in a relentless fight against any sign of aging such as wrinkles, graying at the temples, drying of the skin, loss of vision, or decline in physical/mental aptitude, *etc. ad nauseum*. Popular methods for avoiding these signs of our mortality include exercise regimes, miracle diets, meditation, use of cosmetics, and plastic surgery. Everywhere we look, in popular magazines, news outlets, television, and the movies, we see evidence of our cultural emersion in the "youth movement". Popular articles that I have seen recently range from advice as to: "Exercise Programs for Fabulous Abs" to "Drinking Wine to Reverse the Aging Process". The problem of pursuing this youth movement was put into perspective by Ms. Eloise Hazel who sat next to my daughter while attending a seminar concerning this subject. The speaker at the seminar claimed that the use of his skin care method would allow the user to appear ten years younger. Ms. Hazel whispered to my daughter: "Wow! Wouldn't it be grand to look 70 again?" It is not much consolation to know that we will at least look good in the coffin. If we can't accomplish the trick of looking young through any other method, at least maybe the undertaker can restore our appearance of vitality (irony in its highest form?). Apparently, as the movie *Bernie* indicates, undertakers who can accomplish this feat are in demand.[22] It

21 *Mirror Mirror*, 2012, film directed by Tarsem Singh, starring Lily Collins, Julia Roberts, Armie Hammer, Nathan Lane, and Sean Bean, based on *Schneewittchen und die sieben Zwerge (Snow White and the Seven Dwarfs)*, 1812, The Brothers Grimm (Jacob and Wilhelm).

22 *Bernie*, 2011, film directed by Richard Linklater, written by Linklater and Skip Hollandsworth, starring Jack Black, Shirley MacLaine, and Matthew McConaughey based on a 1998 Texas Monthly magazine article by Hollandsworth, *Midnight in the Garden of East Texas*.

is interesting that, as the name of another movie implies, we maintain the fixation on youth all the way to the grave even though "death may not become us".[23]

The Seventh Tax: Night Moves.[24] Romance, much like other forms of exhilaration, is a peculiar mix of emotions that can be characterized as bittersweet. Romantic attraction is unsettling because romance is rooted in the insecurity that the intensity of the love experienced is somehow proportional to the potential for loss. Perhaps the greatest romantic attraction is associated with the greatest potential catastrophe of imminent death of the loved one. Although romance is considered by most people as the expression of a desired emotion, for many it may be a toss-up as to whether the warm and fuzzy quality felt is offset by the necessity of the threat of accompanying tragedy. Maybe we are more enthralled with the concept of romance than the actual experience of it. This may be the basis of the large pulp fiction, romance novel industry that makes up the majority of paperback novels sold in the United States.[25] The classic romance as epitomized by Shakespeare's *Romeo and Juliet*[26] or, more recently the book and film *Gone with the Wind*[27]. These classics draw a clear link between the intensity of love and the tragedy of loss, and this link is the template for the romance genre. In the modern era, this syndrome may be related to the condition we call commitment phobia.

---

23 *Death Becomes Her*, 1992, film directed by Robert Zemeckis, starring Goldie Hahn, Meryl Streep and Bruce Willis.

24 "Ain't it funny how the night moves, When you just don't seem to have as much to lose, Strange how the night moves, With autumn closing in" *Night Moves*, 1976, written and sung by Bob Seger and the Silver Bullet Band, album *Night Moves*.

25 55% of paperback novels in 2004 were romantic novels. http://en.wikipedia.org

26 *Romeo and Juliet*, 1597, William Shakespeare.

27 *Gone with the Wind*, 1939, film produced by David O. Selznick, directed by Victor Fleming from a screenplay by Sidney Howard, starring Clark Gable and Vivien Leigh, adapted from the book *Gone with the Wind*, 1936, Margaret Mitchell.

This condition results from an inner conflict between the failure to decide between two competing lifestyles, both rooted in the self-awareness of our impermanent condition: on one hand, we want to "live for today", not burdened down with the baggage of family; on the other hand, we feel the urgent need to merge with a true lover (because our "biological clock is ticking") so that we can experience the true bliss of family and children before we are too old.[28] This form of self-taxation might also be called lovesickness or heartbreak and results in the continual unsettledness associated with always being torn between two "good" but conflicting lifestyles, each rooted in the "mortality problem". The tax is experienced in the form of perpetually being on the "horns of a dilemma".

The Eighth Tax: No Fool Like an Old Fool.[29] We take comfort in the fact that life expectancy has markedly increased during the last two centuries as a result of advances in the quality of living conditions and in medicine. During this period of time science has truly transformed our lives, giving grounds for belief that much more is possible. Some scientists have even been so bold as to make the alluring statement that, within the lifespan of people living now, science will advance to the extent that we "will be able to live virtually forever".[30] We have expanded on this hope to the extent that we have invented a new scientific discipline called gerontology. This discipline is dedicated to discovering methods to extend the life span, especially the extension of the portion of life characterized by vim, vigor, and vitality. This line of thought has led to a new way of acting called "amortality: freedom to not act your age".[31] Previously, this freedom was seen, less euphemistically, as the freedom to

28 *He's Scared, She's Scared*, 1993, Steven Carter and Julia Sokol, Dell Publishing, New York, NY, ISBN 0-440-50625-5.

29 "But there is no foole to the olde foole, folke saie." in *Dialogue of Proverbs* II. ii. F4, 1546, J. Heywood.

30 Citation of Ronald Klantz' book *Advances in Anti-aging Medicine* in *Long for this World*, 2010, Jonathon Weiner, ISBN 978-0-06-076536-1.

31 "Amortality, why acting your age is a thing of the past", April, 2011, Catherine Mayer, *Time* Magazine.

act like "an old fool". Recent work at the Mayo Clinic involving cleansing the body of senescent cells has provided some tangibility to the hope that man's lifespan can be expanded markedly in the near future.[32] Others hope to observe the habits of the elderly to gain insight into how not to die.[33] Although the processes put forward in this new science are rooted in an understanding of physiology, the hope expressed in them may be as futile as that guiding the ancient methodology involved in the alchemy of the elixir of life. This hope is pervasive among cultures as indicated by its other names: the philosopher's stone, amrita, ambrosia or nectar depending on the culture.[34] We would like to believe these noble goals are attainable. But, if they are not, the search may be only an exercise in futility and an extension of the form of death tax made famous by Ponce de Leon's search for the fountain of youth, a trap for the credulous, ironically, a waste of time.

The Ninth Tax: Hiding your Head in the Sand. Although the experiences listed here are common to us, we don't necessarily, at least on the surface, associate them with a preoccupation with transience, the fear of mortality. However, if we force ourselves to exhaustive evaluation, the connections are apparent. But, we don't like to let our mortal status rise to our consciousness unless we are forced into it. Therefore, we commonly experience the unsettling emotions described herein but rarely attribute them to our sub-current occupation with our mortality. We do not want to confront this problem. We subconsciously disconnect our drive to amount to something, our belief that we deserve to experience the high life, and our preoccupation with youth (as well as the other forms of the tax) from our controversy with our mortality. Our adamant resistance to any indication that we are controlled by our "mortality syndrome" is evidenced by the fact that, even though violent

32 "Purging Bad Cells Might Delay Aging", Nov. 3, 2011, Nicholas Wade, *New York Times* as reported in the *San Antonio Express-News*.

33 "The Blue Zones: Lessons for Living Longer from the People Who've Lived the Longest", 2008, Dan Buettner, *National Geographic*, ISBN 1426202741.

34 http://en.wikipedia.org

death pervades the media especially through graphic representation of violence in movies, our personal mortality is almost a taboo subject in our culture. An example of this is the recent action of the New York Public School System who took the bold step of publishing a list of topics that are deemed unacceptable for discussion in the public schools. The list included "cancer, crime, divorce and...death".[35] It is ironic that if someone mentions mortality in a discussion, that person is considered to be "morbid". We are adept at developing ingenious ways to escape our personal controversy with death. A common way is to drink away our sorrows. We can also use a variety of mind altering drugs to avoid the issue. The method can be as simple as submerging ourselves in our work. If we are intently occupied with our vocation, we can avoid the issue directly because we are too busy, or indirectly because we are too tired. The tax we pay for escape is made clear in Jimmy Buffett's song: we end up "wastin away again in Margaritaville".[36] This dilemma embodies the tax we pay for escaping a confrontation with our mortality issue.

The Tenth Tax: Bypassing the Toll Road. Our active avoidance of our mortality issue may be one of the reasons that we find attending funerals to be (at least vaguely) unsettling. If we can be honest with ourselves, we must admit that at least a part of the grief we feel upon the loss of a dear one is due to the remorse brought on by the unavoidable reminder that we too will die. John Donne captured the thought when he said, "any man's death diminishes me, because I am involved in mankinde, therefore, never send to know for whom the bell tolls; it tolls for thee".[37] But, we are like Scarlet O'Hara in the film, *Gone with the Wind*[38] that, by

35 "Dinosaurs Too Inflammatory for Words", April 6, 2012, Esther J. Cepeda, the *San Antonio Express-News*.

36 *Margaritaville*, 1977, written and sung by Jimmy Buffett in album *Changes in Latitudes, Changes in Attitudes*.

37 *Meditation XVII Devotions upon Emergent Occasions*, 1624, John Donne.

38 *Gone with the Wind* , 1939, film produced by David O. Selznick, directed by Victor Fleming from a screenplay by Sidney Howard, starring Clark Gable and Vivien Leigh, adapted from the book *Gone with the Wind*, 1936, Margaret Mitchell.

its very name, exudes fear of mortality. She said, in effect, that we don't have to think about that today; if we do we will go crazy. We can think about that tomorrow. When I was growing up, my family showed steers in 4-H at the State Fair of Texas in Dallas. Traveling to the fairgrounds required negotiating the crowded Metroplex. One could travel either the new express toll road, or the old U.S. 80 that amounted to just another street. In the autumn of 1964, I made this trip with my uncle Raymond Holloway, who never wasted a nickel on frivolities such as toll roads. So, whereas my cousins traveling separately chose the new four-lane toll road, Uncle Raymond and I slogged it out on the tried and true old U.S. 80 in his 1960 model Ford half ton pickup, pulling a stock trailer with eight prized steers on board. My cousin's trip took 30 minutes while our "scenic route" exacted an extra two hours because we stopped at most of the 150 intruding traffic lights. When we finally reached the fairgrounds, it was dark. As we unloaded the steers, we discovered that a steer Uncle Raymond knew would be Grand Champion was crippled. Uncle Raymond could never buy into the theory promulgated by the fair's veterinarian that all that stop-go action had triggered a crippling arthritis. Even feeding the steer Grand Prize beer didn't relieve his condition. We avoided the $1.50 toll, but forfeited the Grand Prize. There is a tax to pay, even if we can manage to avoid paying the official toll. As shown in this paragraph, the word "toll" can be used both as an adjective as in the "toll road", or as a verb as in the "tolling of a bell". The word "toll" is etiologically derived from the Latin, *tolones* but has a Greek root: *telones* originally referring to the collection of taxes.[39] Thus "a toll road" means one must pay a tax in order to use the road, and "for whom the bell tolls" means that the ringing of the bell is a summons to pay a tax for living. That tax is death and the emotional strain associated with the anticipation of death. As we have seen, we can avoid paying

39 "toll" from *telones (telos* = goal, *oneomai* = the price): the goal of the tax collector was to determine the quantity of the tax that could be excised from each potential taxpayer. *The Complete Word Study New Testament with Parallel Greek*, 1992, Spiros Zodhiates, AMG Intl., Chattanooga, TN, ISBN 0-89957-652-4.

this tax through elaborate mechanisms of escape, but these mechanisms come with their own tax schedule involving subclinical emotional and sometimes physical strain. Unmanaged stress is a primary cause of the number one killer of Americans: heart disease.[40]

The Eleventh Tax: High Anxiety.[41] In terms of life events that impact us, our problem is that we have "irreconcilable differences with mortality".[42] These irreconcilable differences destabilize our mental condition. We call the chronic form of the destabilization caused by these irreconcilable differences, anxiety. The acute form we call panic. Sometimes we feel the destabilizing effect as a nonspecific, generalized dread that we often cannot associate with any particular cause. Other times such as when our lives are threatened, we experience well defined panic. Since I was raised in west Texas where there is little water, I never was around water deeper than my head. Therefore, I never had the need, nor did I ever learn, to swim. I found my panic point one day a few years ago when my family was "swimming" in the Nueces River in south Texas. I was wading in chest deep water, when I stepped off in a hole and was suddenly out-of-my-depth being carried away by the current. From my present safe perspective I can say (with some coolness) that the reason I panicked is that I was suddenly involuntarily forced to admit that I was not ready to meet my Maker and explain to Him the quality of my covenant with my mortality. Our struggle with mortality, as well as our attempt to avoid the struggle, taxes us in the form of anxiety. The effect of our struggle with mortality on our mental state is compounded by our reluctance to address the issue head-on. Instead of facing the issue and risking panic, we mostly choose a chronic, relentless, subliminal preoccupation

---

40 In 2011, heart disease killed 599,413 Americans; cancer killed the second largest number: 567,628, http://www.cdc.gov. "Stress and Heart Disease", http://www.webmd.com

41 *High Anxiety*, 1977, film produced and directed by Mel Brooks, starring Mel Brooks.

42 "Marriage, Divorcing while Dying", *Time* magazine, February 15, 2010, Belinda Luscombe.

with the problem. Therefore, it is not surprising that the number one mental disease in America has been reported to be anxiety disorder, encumbering more than 12 million Americans.[43]

The Twelfth Tax: Death's Got a Warrant.[44] If we cannot accomplish a clean escape from the foreboding expectation of the inevitability of death, then it seems that the only other possibility is to suffer under a cloud of doom, becoming increasingly despondent as we live. Some find this to be too much to bear. They may escalate and intensify their search for increasingly radical avenues for escape, the most radical being suicide. The alternative is to live under a cloud of doom resulting from the realization of the inevitability of death. This is, perhaps surprisingly, the underlying thought expressed in the phrase "we all have our demons".[45] Although the etiology of the English word demon is not clear, many believe that the word transliterates the Greek, *daimon*, a compound of the root *da* which means to know (the future) and thus be fatalistic and the root *men* which means to be seduced by...[46] We all have our demons; we are all seduced by the fear of our impending death. The associated unsettledness underlies almost everything we do. If we can submerge the demons into our subconsciosness, then we must pay the tax associated with the escape mechanism we choose. Regardless of the mechanism chosen, this escape amounts to living a lie. The attendant tax required for living a lie, as detailed above, can be summed up as living in guilt, fear and doubt, baggage that prevents us from living boldly,

43 Untitled editorial in *Time* magazine, December 7, 2009.

44 "You can't hide, Because you don't know how, Death's got a warrant out for you", *Death's Got a Warrant*, 2010, written by Patty Griffin, sung by Regina McCrary and Ann McCrary, album *Downtown Church*:

45 *We all have Demons*, 2009, album written and sung by The Color Morale: Garret Rapp, Ramon Mendoza, John Bross, Justin Hieser and Steve Carey.

46 *Daimon* is translated as demon in the New Testament. *The Complete Word Study New Testament*, 1994, Spiros Zodiates, AMG Intl. Inc., ISBN 0-89957-652-4 and *A Comprehensive Dictionary of the Original Greek Words with their Precise Meanings for English Readers*, 1947, W.E. Vine, MacDonald, McLean, VA, ISBN 0-917006-03-8.

graciously and confidently. If no satisfactory escape mechanism can be executed, then the cumulative effect of the resulting unsettledness often is despondency.

A Pandemic. We may think that we each uniquely struggle with these dilemmas/issues. The accumulated literature of every culture in the world, however, indicates that the struggle is universal for mankind. This struggle has been addressed by many poets and scholars through time, but maybe the most penetrating statement ever made about our personal struggle with our mortality was written about 2000 years ago by the apostle Paul in his letter to the Romans (Romans 9:33-10:11). In this letter, Paul provided focus for the deeply profound comment on the "mortality problem" written about 700 years before Paul in the great Isaiah scroll. Isaiah 28 describes our response to the problem by providing the insight that all men, probably without even realizing it, make a personal contract with their mortality. The author of Isaiah 28 refers to this contract as our "Covenant with Death" and our "Agreement with Hell". It is in the context of our personal contract with mortality (our Covenant with Death) that the death tax (our Agreement with Hell) must be paid. As shown above, the death tax is a peculiar tax that, unlike our inheritance tax, we do not "pay" at our death, but during our life. The currency of the death tax is also peculiar. It is an emotional tax that results in a diminished quality of life at the least and, at the most, catastrophe. It is also peculiar in that it is a self-imposed tax that we voluntarily charge ourselves. But, its most peculiar trait is that we are adept at making the contract, paying the tax, and then conveniently "forgetting" about it, hiding the contract from ourselves. We notice the tax as we live, but fail to associate the tax with our covert covenant. We routinely condemn the actions associated with the tax, calling these actions "sin" while at the same time extolling the virtues of the root of the problem, our Covenant with Death. We reinforce this covenant by emphasizing the urgency of our life on this earth. This reinforcement occurs through constant reminders, oftentimes from the pulpit, that life is short, and today is the day to act. At the same time, we condemn the manifestations of this urgency that wreck our lives and prevent us from living graciously and boldly, thereby thwarting our ability to live as true pioneers fearlessly confronting the final frontier, the Edge of life.

CHAPTER 2

THE COVENANT WITH DEATH: THE EDGE EFFECT

Sojourners, Romans 9:30-32[47]

"I'm just a wandering on the face of this earth
Meeting so many people
Who are trying to be free..."

I'm Just a Singer (In a Rock and Roll Band), 1972, written by John Lodge, sung by The Moody Blues.

Travelers, Romans 9:30-32. In the early chapters of Romans, Paul describes the law in terms of life's journey. The law is the guardrail keeping the traveler from plummeting over the cliff. As Paul builds toward his *remez* exposing the ramifications of the Covenant with Death (Romans 9:32-10:11), he continues the journey image by describing the kinds of travelers who make life's journey. Paul climaxes this journey motif with Romans 9:32. Usually, journeying is a more dangerous activity than staying at home, especially if the journey is in unknown (or uncharted) territory. It

47 Romans 9 "30 What shall we say then? That the Gentiles, which followed not after righteousness, have attained to righteousness, even the righteousness which is of faith. 31 But Israel, which followed after the law of righteousness, hath not attained to the law of righteousness. 32 Wherefore? Because they sought it not by faith, but as it were by the works of the law. For they stumbled at that stumblingstone;"

goes without saying that getting lost is a major issue, especially if there is no guide to help the traveler get his bearings. I have found that it is ironic that I need GPS based guidance systems the most when traveling in areas where there are no consistent signals allowing my devices to access the systems. GPS can be a useful traveling tool if it can be accessed, but it is also important to have a good guide who knows the way and understands local customs. I have traveled in the mountains of western China visiting nomadic sheep herders, but only under the guidance of Dr. Wu Jianping of the Gansu Agricultural University. With him, I have been able to go places that were not on the map (GPS or otherwise). He was also able to inform me of local customs that might not seem important but could have unforeseen bearing on travel. In traveling these remote, desert, wintery, high mountains, we negotiated many blind, hairpin turns on gravel roads that had no guardrails. I did not need to lean out the window to see straight down to the dry winding river bed far below. I noticed that as we made these turns, the driver never slowed down, but always rolled down his window, and honked. For the first time in my life, I was in a car on a narrow gravel road making hairpin turns at 50 mph without the benefit of guard rails or the ability to see oncoming trucks. After making several of these turns in succession and meeting several overloaded trucks that were as wide as the road, when I gathered enough nerve to open my eyes, I ventured to ask Dr. Wu why, when it was snowing, we didn't roll up the windows. He replied that if we rolled up the windows we could not hear the warning honk of trucks approaching on the other side of the turn.

Wanderers, Romans 9:30. The image is of travelers, Jews and Gentiles on journeys across generations or, of more pertinence to us, any man's journey through life. The picture painted in Romans 9:30 is of the Gentiles stumbling along in the dark on their journey to nowhere. They were more like "just driving around" or "joy riding" than being intent on going somewhere. When I was growing up, a common practice for young people in Merkel (as well as in many other communities at the time) was to drive around the local "drag". You didn't actually go anywhere, but it gave you something to do; we called it "dragging Main Street". This can become a pattern of life as Paul depicted for the Gentiles. They were in the dark because they did not avail themselves to the light (not seeking God's rightness). Most travelers in ancient times tried to journey in the daytime so they could at least see the perils of the road such as landslides, robbers and detours. At night, anything could happen, including getting lost or murdered.[48] The Gentiles are depicted as lackadaisical travelers stumbling along blindly. Surprisingly and fortuitously, they looked up one day and discovered that they somehow had arrived at the destination intended for them. This was surprising because they had no destination in mind when they began their journey. They had not sought this destination but without really knowing it, they stumbled upon something so attractive that, in retrospect, they labeled it their destination, trying to make everyone believe that it was their goal all along. After arrival, they did, to their credit, recognize it for its inherent value. They had stumbled on the light.[49] When they arrived, again to their credit, they became strongly connected to their newfound destination, gained confidence in it. They felt at home in it.[50]

God Wrestlers, Romans 9:31-32. The Jews are depicted in Romans as serious travelers who are purposeful in their travels.[51] In contrast

---

48 Romans 9:30 "the Gentiles"...*ethnee*, [English: ethnic] ***The rabble*** "which followed not after righteousness": *meh* = ***possibly not***, *diokonta* = present active participle of *dioko*, ***persistently and urgently pursuing***...*dikaiosuneen* = aorist participle active of *dikaosune*, ***being right with God, walking in His light...***

49 Romans 9:30 "have attained to righteousness", *katelaben*, aorist indicative active of *katalambano*, ***somehow, eagerly seized...dikaiosuneen*** = ***the condition of rightness with God...***, having the light required to continue on the straight and narrow, being on the level, going straight...

50 Romans 9:30 "of faith", *ek pisteoos*, ***out of confidence, being able to confide in the family*** [one can feel free to confide in someone if they are confident, at ease, feeling at home, a feeling of belonging]...

51 Romans 9:31, "Israel" *Ysrahale* = ***Those who would rule as the Almighty***, originally named Jacob [Genesis 32:35-38], *Ya*^{a}*qob* = the supplanter who wrestled [*b*^{a}*hee'aabqow*, Genesis 32:28, Niphal {passive} infinitive construct of *awbak'* = to grapple] with God. "followed after the law of righteousness", *diokoon* = present active participle of the same root [*diooko*] as the verb used to describe the Gentiles in their search for nothing, ***are persistently and continually, taking matters in their own hands, attempting to right themselves with God...***

to the Gentiles, the Jews were in strict attendance to the goal of the journey.[52] They were seeking after "the law of righteousness". The root of the Greek word for righteousness has a certain ambiguity about it, allowing for possibly either a positive or a negative motive. So, they might not have been doing the right thing because they wanted to "do good for goodness sake" as much as they were driven to do good because they feared the consequence of the alternative (such as plummeting down a cliff).[53] They were also sticklers for the warning signs along the road, thereby becoming enthralled with the process of the journey,[54] losing sight of their destination, ultimately coming to a confidence crisis. They lost confidence that their destination even existed and, if it did, they had no confidence in its nature.[55] Ironically, they were ultimately impeded by the very goal they were seeking when they began their journey. The happiest event of their journey should have been their arrival at their destination. Instead, their destination wasn't what they had expected. They came upon it unawares and it was a painful experience.[56] The

---

52 Romans 9:"31 the law of righteousness" [***the goal of the journey was...***] *nomon* = ***the allotment of equity*** as exemplified by the nomadic parceling of grazing, allowing the animals a certain pasturage [an image used to depict the principle of a matter] defined by the pastor, who in this case was guided by *dikaiosunees* = desiring equity with God, ***denoting the condition of acceptability with God...***

53 Upon further investigation of *nomon dikaiosunees*, we discover that their motives might not be as positive as we might have first thought. Recapping, we can say that they were ***actively pursuing it, even if their motives were negative...*** [the root of *diooko* is *deos* = fearful dread, journeying more from the motive of fleeing something feared rather than from the motive of eagerly pursuing something desired].

54 Romans 9:31 "the works of the law", *hoos ex ergoon* = ***out of the toil*** or business... [busyness], through their strong work ethic, the word for law was not in many original manuscripts.

55 "not by faith", *ouk ek pisteoos*, ***absolutely not out of their confidence in the guarantee*** [*pisteoos* as defined as faith or confidence is equated to a guarantee], according to the guarantee [based on faith/confidence] that their destination actually exists...

56 Romans 9:32, "stumbled at that stumblingstone", *prosekopsan* = ***they tripped on the...****litho* = ***stone marker they had overlooked but which had stubbed their toe...****tou proskommatos* = aorist indicative active of *proskopto* [*pros* = toward, *kopto* = to chop, cut] ***causing them pain...***

bottom line is that they "hath not attained to the law of righteousness". They did arrive at the goal of their journey, but they failed to recognize it as their destination.[57] How tragic a condition for serious travelers who followed the "rules of the road" meticulously, getting all the style points, never getting a ticket, never running off the road, always going the speed limit, but losing their way, never consciously arriving at their destination, but not realizing that they had lost their way. This is a picture of the stereotype of the male of our species traveling without the benefit of a woman's willingness to admit to being lost and stopping to ask for directions. The journey just goes on and on interminably.

Illustration 1, A Personal Problem. The journey may lead beside the still waters (Psalms 23:2). Path along Sea of Galilee toward the Horns of Hattin (left), footprints in the "salty sand" along the Dead Sea (right).

A Personal Problem, Romans 9:30-32. These two scenarios also characterize possible courses of our lives. Most of us are like the Gentiles in Romans 9:30[58] as we lackadaisically stumble through life not actively searching for the truth, only discovering it through, what seems to us, as serendipity. The other possibility (Romans 9:31-32)[59] may alternatively characterize some. It involves attacking life's journey purposefully, but becoming enthralled with the mechanics of the journey. These lose sight

57 Romans 9:31, "hath not attained the law of righteousness", *ouk ethasesn, ouk* = ***absolutely did not***...*ethasen* = aorist indicative active of *phthano* = anticipate or ***arrive at the principles of right standing with God***...

58 Romans 9:30"the Gentiles"...*ethnee*, ***the rabble...***

59 Romans 9:31, "Israel" *Ysrahale* = ***he will rule as the Almighty***...

of their goal because they fail to anticipate its character, thereby failing to recognize it when they stumble on it. I have driven by destinations before because I had developed in my mind visions of what the destinations must look like. When they didn't have an appearance consistent with my expectations, I drove by them without knowing it. As my mother would have said, "If they had been snakes, they would have bit you". Jesus in John 14:1-4 extended this journey image beyond this life. The incorporation of the awareness of this extension into our lifestyle is the secret for the success of our journey. The climax of the journey is the stumbling of the serious traveler on the stumblingstone or, as we shall see, for the more casual traveler, the fortuitous discovery of the Cornerstone. Because we are journeymen traveling on a road punctuated by the edges of birth and death, we feel forced to "make our peace" with the stark realities of the journey, including the fact that all journeys have destinations, and the fact that all journeys on this earth are finite in duration. Thus, because we are travelers, we feel that we must make a deal with our mortality. Many of us become enthralled with the journey itself and lose track of God's goal for the journey. We become attached to the journey through our preoccupation with our mortality. Or, another way of looking at it is that because we are permanently occupied with our mortality, we lose our vision of the real destination of our journey. We become too focused on trying to stay young or trying to leave a legacy to pay much attention to following the true pioneer to God's goal for us. As a professor at the University of Tennessee for ten years, I found that many of the students to whom I was faculty advisor, like I was at their age, had no clear vision of what they wanted to be. We were like the Gentiles in Romans 9, wandering about, trying to find our way while studiously avoiding any guidance provided by authoritarians. It is the fortunate person that comes upon a worthy goal before it is too late in life to live out the goal. It is the fortunate person who can find a worthy lifetime goal (transcending death's door), allowing avoidance of the all-consuming efforts required in working out a private deal (a covenant) with death.

A Very Personal Problem, Romans 9:30-32. My mother was always a Baptist. She grew up in a Baptist family in a part of Oklahoma seemingly always blessed with rain. She even had a Biblical name, Naomi.[60] My daddy came by religion the hard way. He grew up in a family that frequented saloons not churches, living on a stock farm near a place that was then almost as wild as its name, Buffalo Gap, Texas. They "met" as "pen pals" while daddy fought in the European Theater of World War II. My mother instigated the relationship because she was attracted to daddy's family name; it was the same as her maiden name: Holloway. The source of the name is in dispute but could have originated in antiquity from the association of the family with an old road connecting London to a religious shrine. This road was called the "hallowed way". The other possible alternative for the origin of the name is that the road could have gone through a hollow and been called the "hollow way".[61] Regardless, as soon as the war was over and my mother met and married daddy, she began to try to lead him down the "hallowed way". It was a long road, taking 50 years of (sometimes not so pleasant) persuasion, but persistence paid off. Back in the early days, mother would usually make a strong effort to persuade daddy to attend the revival services of the Missionary Baptist Church in Stith, Texas about ten miles from our farm. Stith consisted of about four homesteads, a cotton gin (and associated domino hall) and the white-framed church house. Revivals were held in the open-air Tabernacle in a field next to the church. Historically, revivals in west Texas were held as "tent meetings" each summer; the Tabernacle was a step up from the traditional tent. It was cooler than the stuffy church especially as augmented by handheld cardboard fans supplied free of charge by a funeral home (seems fitting somehow). The Tabernacle had a dirt floor, cedar posts holding up the tin roof, and strings of bare, yellow-bulb lights providing "bug-proof" lighting for the services that could go well into the night. There was a podium for the circuit evangelist, a "tinny" piano and wooden benches for the more rigorous participants such as my mother. Those having a more casual interest, such as my daddy, could sit in their cars and pickups in rows facing the Tabernacle and "listen". That way, if the preacher got too personal,

60 Ruth 1:2, *Naa[a]miy*, pleasant.

61 Either those who lived near a sunken road, a hollow way, or near a road to a religious shrine, a holy way, http://www.houseofnames.com

they could turn up the radio so that music from the Sons of the Pioneers on *WSM* would be the dominant signal. That way, daddy had the choice of going the hallowed way or his way (the hollow way?). One doesn't want to get tied down to a way, especially if he doesn't know where he is going.

The Best Hope, Romans 9:33a, Isaiah 28:14[62]

"Now Ev'ry gambler knows that the secret to survivin'
Is knowin' what to throw away and knowing what to keep.
'Cause ev'ry hand's a winner and ev'ry hand's a loser,
And the best that you can hope for is to die in your sleep."

The Gambler, 1978, written by Don Schlitz, sung by Kenny Rogers and Bobby Bare.

It Is Just a Rock, Romans 9:33a. A methodical approach is required to understand Paul's use of the stumblingstone/Cornerstone metaphor in his journey imagery. First, I will explore his use of the "stone" metaphor. The characterization of God's waymarker for life's journey (or, as those enamored with the journey perceive it, the impediment to life's journey) as a stone is rather difficult to get our minds around. The concept is not in our common parlance and is difficult to comprehend in all its aspects. In the verses between the two references to Isaiah 28 (Romans 9:33-10:11), Paul amplifies the meaning of God's response to our Covenant with Death and the meaning of the Cornerstone. Paul signals to the reader that this discussion is an amplification of Isaiah 28 by referring to Isaiah 28:16 in both Romans 9:33 and 10:11. First, Paul begins his amplification (allusion, *remez*) by referring to how this stone came to our attention in the first place through God's ancient action at the mountain that the Jews knew as signal mountain, Mount Zion. It was known as signal mountain because it was the lower hill

62 Romans 9:33a "As it is written, Behold, I lay in Sion a stumblingstone and rock of offence." Isaiah 28:14 "Wherefore hear the word of the LORD, ye scornful men, that rule this people which is in Jerusalem."

of two seemingly related hills.[63] Sighting from it up to the other taller hill points to the sky, ostensibly the eternal bode of God. Sighting the other way, from the taller hill down to the lower, provides a view of a stone (or now, the temple housing the stone), the stone on which the elderly Abraham was to sacrifice his son Isaac, but instead sacrificed a ram. It is this stone that Paul describes in Romans 9:33a. A stone is a common sight along a road in Palestine. I will defer the exploration of God's intention in planting the rock in our paths until the discussion of Isaiah 28:16, but, for now, I will explore how this rock can affect the traveler adversely.

Traveler's Warning: The Tar Baby Syndrome, Romans 9:33a. This particular stone is not one of your run-of-the-mill rocks that, by chance, lies along the path, vulnerable to accidental contact with travelers. According to Paul, this stone has two salient characteristics. First, the stone is called a "stumblingstone". A stumblingstone is a stone with character that impedes travel. This impediment causes the traveler grief, demanding that he give it greater scrutiny.[64] Close examination leads to the discovery of the second characteristic of the stone, an amplification

---

63 Romans 9:33a, "Behold" *Idou* = ***I must call attention to a surprise...*** "I lay" *tithemi*, present indicative active: ***I put in place...*** "in Sion" *en tseeyone* = ***in the guiding monument***, waymark, a signal as a mile marker, conspicuous prominence, the place where God provided a ram to free Isaac from the sacrifice required by God of Abraham (Genesis 22:13)... It is the place also known as Jerusalem, *Yeruwshalah'im* = a duality, in reference to its two main hills, one taller than the other as if begging the observer to line his sight toward something [the sky?], *Yeruwshalah'im* is a compound word of the passive participle of *yawraw'* = to have it pointed out to you, and *shawlam'* = safety, security, peace, *The New Strong's Exhaustive Concordance of the Bible*, 1990, James Strong, Thomas Nelson Publishers, Nashville, TN, ISBN 0-8407-6750-1,

64 Romans 9:33, "stumblingstone", *lithon* = ***a cut stone, cut for a purpose*** [from the same root as the English word for a stone made useful by providing a surface for writing, the lithograph, a stone for engraving]. But, the next word in the phrase describes the perceived purpose of the *lithon*: *proskommatos* = toward the chop, ***a token of grief***; this adverse purpose gives it a perverse quality...

of the first: it is called a "rock of offense".[65] Ultimately, the traveler is offended merely by the presence of the rock. The Greek word translated as "offense" is the root of the English word, scandal and, in its original meaning, indicates that the traveler becomes trapped by the rock. Since an inanimate object lying by the road can't entrap a passer-by, something else is involved. The traveler is actually trapped, not by the rock itself, but by his reaction to the rock. He is caught up in his own thoughts about the stone and thus he himself (not the rock itself) is the reason he does not make progress on his journey. What impedes the traveler is his fixation on the startling idea that the rock did not happen to be in the path by chance. The traveler comes to the conclusion that the rock was planted and that the one who planted it apparently had a malevolent intent in mind. That intent apparently was to throw a future traveler off course. The traveler responds to an inanimate object in an emotional manner because he takes the planting of the rock as a personal affront. Confrontation with this rock, oddly enough, narrows his alternatives in journeying.[66] This is the picture of Brer Bear and Brer Fox in their attempt to entrap Brer Rabbit with the Tar Baby. Brer Rabbit became entangled with the Tar Baby, not so much because of the Tar Baby's character, but because of his own assumptions and emotions.[67] Because of Brer Rabbit's heated interaction with the Tar Baby, he became inextricably entwined with it so that he could not escape on his own. If the traveler can escape entrapment by the stone but can notice it as to its potential danger, then the stone can be considered from a benign perspective. If viewed in that

65 Romans 9:33, "a rock", *petron* = ***a massive rock,*** larger than *lithon*, its projecting tip could appear small at first glance until the traveler tries to kick it out of the way, in which case, the traveler finds it well-placed, a formidable, integral instrument, a constituent of the whole, a protrusion of bedrock...

66 Romans 9:33 "of offense" translates *skandalou* = ***a trap,*** snare, scandal, technically the trigger of the trap upon which the bait is placed, thus providing the basis for a lure into error. This definition involves the anticipated conduct of the prey: trapped and enticed, with the anticipated outcome of binding, narrowing its range of possibilities, encumbering it...

67 *Uncle Remus: His Songs and His Sayings*, 1881, Joel Chandler Harris, D. Appleton and Co., New York, NY.

light it can serve as a waymarker or a warning signal, or perhaps, even a Cornerstone. In the context of Isaiah 28, the warning concerns the dangers (taxes) that accrue as the result of our Covenant with Death.

Mixed Metaphors, Isaiah 8, 28. But, if Paul is referring to Isaiah 28 in Romans 9:33 as he seems to be in that he quotes *verbatim* Isaiah 28:16a, "Behold I lay in Sion", shouldn't he have used the term "Cornerstone"? The use of the term "stumblingstone" seems out of place, a flashback to Isaiah 8. Through the use of signal words in Romans 9:32-33, Paul is calling to mind for students of his *remez* the combined thoughts of chapters 8 and 28 of Isaiah. Isaiah 8 refers to the stumblingstone[68] in contempt, not of God, but of the way Israel viewed God in comparison to the real role of God. His real role is to provide the Cornerstone, the only safe refuge available for journeymen.[69] As is the style of Paul, he placed a "bookend" in the text with this reference that he didn't close until Romans 10:11 by referring again to Isaiah 28:16. By setting these "bookends", Paul indicates that the intervening discussion (*remez*) not only extends his prior discussion of "the journey" but also comments upon, and brings focus to, the primary topic of Isaiah 28. This topic embodies the answer to the question Isaiah posed in chapter 8 as to: what does God provide refuge (sanctuary) from? The answer, according to Isaiah 28, is that we need refuge from our Covenant with Death (our private deal with our

---

68 Isaiah 8:14 "And he shall be for a sanctuary;" ***God is called*** the "sanctuary", *l^a^miqdaash* = ***a refuge,*** asylum possibly a reference to the hiding place in the cleft of the rock [Ex 33:22 "And it shall come to pass, while my glory passeth by, that I will put thee in a cleft of the rock, and will cover thee with my hand while I pass by:"] "but for a stone of stumbling", *uwl'eben negep,* ***the people think of Him instead as a*** building ***stone left lying around only good for tripping the unwary,*** "and for a rock of offence", *uwltsuwr mikshowl,* ***specifically, as the edge of a boulder acting as a scruple enticing a traveler to fall,*** "to both the houses of Israel, for a gin" *l^a^pach,* spring net, "***and acting as a snare*** to the inhabitants of Jerusalem." *Uwlmowqeesh,* ***a noose.***

69 Isaiah 28:16: "Cornerstone", *aaben bochan pinat,* ***a building stone, examined to be true,*** used at the pinnacle of the building, thereby holding the building together.

mortality) and our Agreement with Hell (the resultant death tax).[70] Before we can address Paul's amplification of the provision for this refuge in the Cornerstone, we must first address this Covenant with Death and the Agreement with Hell described in Isaiah 28.

Travelers Dilemma, Romans 9:33. Romans 9:33 is a pivotal verse connecting three themes: life, travel and being ashamed. Paul says that life is a journey and that journeys predispose journeymen to being tripped up and thereby subjected to potential for embarrassment. In my journeys I have found that travel puts the traveler in unfamiliar situations, allowing for the opportunity to express otherwise suppressed vulnerabilities in terms of embarrassment. I could give many personal examples, but three will suffice concerning trips I have made to various professional meetings with my daughters. I traveled to a cattle meeting in Queensland, Australia with my daughter Amber and my trusted colleague Dr. Bobby Warrington. All went well on the trip until, during our return, through my mistake (I blame jetlag), we lost our luggage at the Los Angeles International Airport. When we retrieved our luggage at LAX baggage claim to go through the U.S. Customs Inspection, my bag was open. I closed it, went through Customs, and put it back into the system without checking it for our destination, San Antonio, Texas. We spent the next two weeks trying to retrieve it. It finally arrived at our small hometown of Uvalde, Texas, three weeks later. It all arrived except for a pillow case with the monogrammed letter "H" that I had used as a hamper for my dirty underwear during the trip; this was missing. We, of course, were willing to sacrifice this small item. But, a week later, I received notice that a package from the airline had arrived at the local bus station. I went to the bus station and, in front of many curious locals, received the pillowcase (complete with dirty underwear) that was only marked with the monogrammed "H" and the encircling yellow tape announcing "inspected by U.S. Customs". On another venture,

---

70 Isaiah 28:15 "covenant with death" *b^arit et maawet,* a compact made together [personally] with death, "and with hell are we in agreement", *w^aim sh^aowl 'aasiynow chozeh',* and with the place of the dead we accomplish our compact for the future.

I traveled to a cattle meeting in Clermont-Ferrand, France with my daughter Brooke. We scheduled a daylong layover in Paris, thinking we could store our luggage at the airport and have time to explore the city. Unfortunately, we were surprised to find, upon our arrival at Orly International Airport that, because of a bomb threat, the airport would not allow baggage to be "checked". Therefore, she and I had to drag our luggage all over the City Centre as we toured. Because of the bomb threat, our luggage was examined every time we visited a public-accessible site. When we boarded a tour boat on the Seine River, Brooke stepped away for a moment, and when she returned, the security guards were in the process of examining some of her more personal apparel. They noticed her return and, while rapidly speaking excited French, showed every indication that they had found something illegal, threatening to jettison her open bag into the Seine. Few times in her life have I found her to be speechless, but this was one of those occasions. On another trip, my daughter Crystal and I went to a cattle meeting in Saskatoon, Canada. During a side visit to Lake Louise in Banff National Park, a glacier-fed, glass-smooth body of turquoise water surrounded by the snow-peaked Rocky Mountains. Although neither of us had ever been in a canoe, we decided to rent one to explore the lake. To say that we had some problems coordinating our efforts is an understatement. After much rowing that mostly sent our craft in circles, we (more or less) washed up on the shore next to the terrace of the Chateau Lake Louise, one of Canada's Grand Railway Hotels where a party was in progress. We were reduced to using our oars as poles to pole our canoe around the shore to the canoe rental dock. Our hopes that we had escaped unnoticed were dashed the next day while we were buying film at the Chateau's gift shop, when the clerk said, "Oh, you are the ones in the canoe yesterday." Since these incidents amply illustrate the possibilities for embarrassment during journeys, it won't be necessary to mention the vehicles I have wrecked in the British Isles trying to drive on the left side of the road while studiously ignoring driving lessons presented to me by my wife Debby. If a person does not want to be subjected to potentially embarrassing situations, I recommend staying at home, possibly hiding under the bed. Since life's journey continually subjects the journeyman to new situations, this is not possible, especially since that journey leads to the Edge.

Resurrection, More than a Hobby,[71] **Isaiah 28.** Isaiah 28:1-18 introduces the agreement (Covenant) that each of us makes with ourselves concerning our mortal condition. As I have said, we usually make this agreement without consciously knowing it. This agreement is important to us because through it we can live our lives with some semblance of sanity in the face of the apparent certainty of our mortality. The only downside is that the Covenant requires payment. To understand what Isaiah meant by the term "Covenant", we need to understand that the author wrote both for an immediate outcome and for a more global, spiritual and personal outcome. The immediate outcome concerned the context of his writing. It is generally thought that Isaiah 28-33 was written during the first years of Hezekiah's reign over the southern kingdom of Judah at the time of the prophet Micah. At that time, Assyria was threatening the northern Jewish kingdom of Israel (*circa* 700 B.C.E.). Ahaz, the king of Israel submitted to Assyria, while Hezekiah allied with Egypt to gain protection from Assyria. Thus, the author of Isaiah 28 refers to these inter-country covenants when he refers to the "Covenant with Death". We know that the author not only had in mind a "local focus" but also a more global and spiritual meaning for the term, because he did not refer to a "covenant with Assyria or with Egypt" but to a "Covenant with Death" (Isaiah 28:15). When we confront this Covenant on a personal basis, we must address the necessity for our personal resurrection in providing perspective in living daily.

Desperate Measures,[72] **Isaiah 28:14.** By covenant, Isaiah was referring to an ancient method of forming alliances signaled by a ceremony of

---

71 From *Skyfall*, 2012, film starring Daniel Craig as Ian Fleming's James Bond 007, Javier Bardem as Silva, directed by Sam Mendes: Bond: "Everybody needs a hobby." Silva: "So, what's yours?" Bond: "Resurrection."

72 *Desperate Measures*,1998, film starring Michael Keaton, Andy García, Marcia Gay Harden and Brian Cox, directed by Barbet Schroeder.

cutting *(b^{a}rit)*.[73] The covenant ceremony usually involved the union of two people of equal but complementary stature. The union was a solemn agreement signifying a merger so complete that the two would become one through the mixing of bloods, in our parlance an agreement signed in blood. The usual reason for forming this union was that the two could accomplish a united, synergistic work through performing an enterprise that neither could perform alone. The agreement was often in the form of a marriage signifying, not only the union of two people, but the union of two families to accomplish an ambitious work. Although this is the most common covenant described in the Old Testament, it is not the kind of *b^{a}rit* discussed in Isaiah 28. The type described in Isaiah 28 was not entered into by two equals with the design of accomplishing an ambitious work, but was a *b^{a}rit* entered into out of desperation by an inferior party with a superior party having the goals of keeping the inferior party viable and enriching the superior party. Such was Israel's covenant with Assyria, Judah's proposed covenant with Egypt, and our Covenant with Death. This kind of covenant usually involved a transfer of property (the tax) required of the inferior party in exchange for the promise of freedom or the sparing of life made by the superior party. The problem with this kind of covenant from the standpoint of the inferior party is that the tax is continual and may escalate over time depending on the whims of the superior party. Who knows whether the superior party (e.g. Assyria) might take the loot and go away, only to return later to renew the siege of the city with renewed demands for more booty. This can become a cloud hanging over the city, causing the residents to live in fear of blackmail and escalating taxation into the future. In the larger, more spiritual scope of the intention of the author of Isaiah 28, man is not in position to bargain with death, just as Israel was not in position to bargain with Assyria. Thus, out of desperation, man is forced to make the best deal he can muster with death. As in the case of Israel, this deal has the downside of an escalating, perpetual taxation and does not ameliorate the fear associated with impending doom. This deal has

73 In Isaiah 28:14, *b^{a}rit* is a Qal perfect tense verb of *kawrath'* meaning "to cut".

the possibility of several flavors. These flavors are vividly described in Isaiah 28:1-18.

Life in the Fast Lane, Isaiah 28:1-8[74]

"There were lines on the mirror, lines on her face.
She pretended not to notice, she was caught up in the race."

Life in the Fast Lane, album *Hotel California,* Joe Walsh, Glenn Frey, Don Henley, 1976, Eagles.

Living on the Fat Plain, Isaiah 28:1-3. When it comes to the trial, when we go before the judge, we can always plead that "We were 'set up'. It wasn't our fault, your Honor; we were lured into a trap." This is the picture painted in Isaiah 28. In this imagery we were lured by the beautiful, bountiful river bottom to build our house in the flood plain. In verse 1 we are introduced to the lure of "the head of the fat valleys".[75] This picture is very appealing because the deep soil in the "fat valley" gives rise to lush crops and thus to prosperity and the promise of the high life. We visualize lazy Sunday afternoons lounging on the veranda

---

74 Isaiah 28: "1 Woe to the crown of pride, to the drunkards of Ephraim, whose glorious beauty is a fading flower, which are on the head of the fat valleys of them that are overcome with wine! 2 Behold, the Lord hath a mighty and strong one, which as a tempest of hail and a destroying storm, as a flood of mighty waters overflowing, shall cast down to the earth with the hand. 3 The crown of pride, the drunkards of Ephraim, shall be trodden under feet. 4 And the glorious beauty, which is on the head of the fat valley, shall be a fading flower, and as the hasty fruit before the summer; which when he that looketh upon it seeth, while it is yet in his hand he eateth it up. 5 In that day shall the LORD of hosts be for a crown of glory, and for a diadem of beauty, unto the residue of his people, 6 And for a spirit of judgment to him that sitteth in judgment, and for strength to them that turn the battle to the gate. 7 But they also have erred through wine, and through strong drink are out of the way; the priest and the prophet have erred through strong drink, they are swallowed up of wine, they are out of the way through strong drink; they err in vision, they stumble in judgment. 8 For all tables are full of vomit and filthiness, so that there is no place clean."

75 Isaiah 28:1, "the head of the fat valleys", the picture of the *ro'sh,* ***the crown...*** *geey,* ***of the flood plain...*** *sh^{a}maariym,* ***of fruit orchards.***

under the spreading oak trees, sipping mint juleps, watching the children play. The promise of the good life played to our weakness, our "crown of pride".[76] Although we were warned early on that there was a reason it was called a fat valley (flood plain), we conveniently "forgot" this when we lost ourselves in our dreams of the high life. After all, we did know from the beginning that its richness was the result of the periodic floods that could be caused by a "tempest of hail and a destroying storm, as a flood of mighty waters overflowing".[77] The picture was all too real for people living in the Middle East, and is most vividly portrayed by the Nile river flood plain that was the "bread basket" for Egypt and the Middle East (including Rome), but its fertility was dependent upon the annual flooding of the great Nile. In years of reduced flooding, the soil was not benefited by the accompanying fertility brought by the new alluvial soil normally laid down by the flood and the crops were less plenteous, but when the flooding was great, people living in the plain were drowned.[78] Life is good and we enjoy living it. We only have to accept one small downside and everything will be wonderful. We have plenty of warning about that downside in life as brought to our attention early in Isaiah 28 as the "glorious beauty is a fading flower".[79] We might be able to convince ourselves that the high life is permanent, except that when we look in the mirror we see evidence that we are changing. (Could it be decay? God forbid.) We can ignore the signs, however, if we can manipulate ourselves

---

76 Isaiah 28:1, "crown of pride", ^{a}*Teret,* ***the reward for...****gee'uwt,* ***our arrogance*** [from *gaw'aw* = self-rising].

77 Isaiah 28:2, "tempest of hail and a destroying storm, as a flood of mighty waters overflowing", *qaaTebsa'ar,* ***is a torrential storm that cuts us off from our planned retreat...***[from *sa'ar* = to shiver in fear] *k*^{a}*zerem,* ***as a flood in a dry wadi...*** *baaraad,* ***accompanied with hail stones that are...****shoT*^{a}*piym,* Qal participle active of *shawtaf,* ***inundating, pounding, frightening because it is out of our control...***

78 *Cleopatra, A Life,* 2010, Stacy Schiff, 2010. Back Bay Books, Little Brown and Company, New York, NY, ISBN 978-0-316-00192-2.

79 Isaiah 28:1, "glorious beauty is a fading flower", *tsebee tiparto,* ***whose prominent, most conspicuous embellishment is...*** *nobeel w*^{a}*tstits,* ***a faint, wilting flower, a small reminder of previous splendor.***

so that we get caught up in the whirlwind of life in the fat valley. We become obsessed with the life in the fast lane, and while we believe we possess it, in reality, we are possessed by it as "them that are overcome with wine".[80] We become intoxicated with the headiness of the fast lane as "the drunkards of Ephraim".[81] But, the downside of the impending doom of the inevitable flood hangs in the offing. Thus, we feel coerced into making a personal deal with our mortality.

Once Is Not Enough,[82] Isaiah 28:4. The lure of the fast lane is heightened by the understanding that the high life is fleeting as a "fading flower".[83] This understanding may exist only in the subconsciousness and, because it causes a pain that we can avoid, we may never openly admit it, even to ourselves. But, as we have seen, this subconscious understanding of transience can be a driver that underlies many problems that we cause ourselves in life. "The hasty fruit before the summer"[84] invokes the picture of the grower who gauges the emergence of the figs as the season progresses, watching daily, eagerly anticipating the sweet fruit, remembering the luscious flavor last experienced nearly a year ago. This describes a more vivid anticipation of sensation than we experience today since we have year-round access to many fresh fruits. The grower also remembers the previous years' experiences that the first fruits are often the tastiest, made even more tasty by the possibility that the first fruits

80 Isaiah 28:1, "them that are overcome with wine", *h^aluwmeey*, Qal participle passive of *hawlam* = ***those being struck down with the hammer of...****yawyin* = ***effervescent, intoxicating wine.***

81 Isaiah 28:3, "the drunkards" *shikowreey* = ***the intoxicated ones,*** under the control of the drink.

82 *Once Is Not Enough*, 1973 novel, Jacqueline Susann, ISBN 0802135455, 1975 film Jacqueline Susann's Once Is Not Enough, directed by Guy Green and starring Kirk Douglas, Deborah Raffin, David Janssen and Brenda Vaccaro.

83 Isaiah 28: 1 and 4, "fading flower", *tsiytsat* = feminine for ***the flower that is...*** *nobeel* = ***wilting, becoming faint, desiccating...***Isaiah emphasizes this theme by returning to the imagery several times in chapter 28.

84 Isaiah 28:4, "The hasty fruit before the summer", *kabikuwraah*, ***the first fruit...*** *b^aterem*, in suspense, ***vulnerable to interruption and to...****qayits*, ***the harvest...***

may be the last. The birds may also be watching the development of the crop, as well as perhaps the neighbors. Then there is the possibility of the hail (Isaiah 28: 2), to say nothing of the worm. The grower must realize that "there is many a slip between the cup and the lip" and worry that the first fruit has a fair chance of being all there is. The effect on the grower is described as "which when he looketh upon it seeth".[85] Since it is not yet ripe, the grower does not consume the fruit, but, as the Hebrew wording indicates, the fruit does consume the grower. The fruit accomplishes this by capturing the grower's attention and imagination in a similar manner as the wine captures the drunkards in Isaiah 28:1, not the other way around. But, it does ripen and, as soon as it does, "while it is yet in his hand he eateth it up". Although in actuality, the grower is consumed by the fruit, it seems to him that he is consuming the fruit.[86]

Grab for all the Gusto,[87] Isaiah 28:4. We know the feeling well. The feeling that the opportune moment for satisfaction is passing us by, that we deserve more than this one moment in the sun, that we have wasted too much time in activities that have not satisfied, and that even though this present satisfaction may not last long, we must "grab for all the gusto" we can. We must "live for today, for tomorrow we may die".[88] We deserve more than our spouse or family or our job is giving us. Therefore, it becomes imperative to trade these for something having the promise of

---

85 Isaiah 28:4, "which when he looketh upon it seeth", *yireh...haaro'eh*, Qal imperfect and Qal participle active verbs of the same root, *ra'ah* = ***When he first begins to see it, it increasingly occupies him and he is in the process of being entranced by it, being enthralled...***

86 Isaiah 28:4, "while it is yet in his hand he eateth it up", *owtaah*, ***It is as a beacon...*** *b^{a}owdaah*, ***that is transient, as it transitions...*** [the fruit is transitioning from ripening to rotting]...*yiblaaenaa*, Qal imperfect of *bawlah* = ***he begins to hastily swallow it whole, gobbling it up...***

87 "You only go around once in this life, so you have to grab for all the gusto you can get." 1971, The Joseph Schlitz Brewing Company now owned by Pabst Brewing Co., Los Angeles, CA.

88 " We'll take the most from living, have pleasure while we can,... live for today," *Let's Live for Today*, 1966, written by David Shapiro, Ivan Mogull, and Michael Julien, initially sung by The Rokes, popularized by The Grass Roots.

being more immediately satisfying. We hope to fulfill a deeper desire now even though we may vomit later, even though this act may do irreparable harm. We don't have to worry about that today; we can worry about that tomorrow, or so said Scarlet O'Hara. The typical form of "hasty fruit" is in sex, mind-altering drugs or alcohol, or even exercise. Through each of these, we can experience a temporary, transient high that provides at least a momentary euphoria and escape from our struggle with mortality. These desires for escape are common to us and constitute a tax resulting from our Covenant with Death.

Illustration 2, A New Gate. Ancient city gates such as this one at Dan (Canaanite Gate: Gate of Three Arches) provided controlled access through the establishment of corners. The Gate of Three Arches as it appears today, left and as it appeared when Abraham rescued Lot, right (Genesis 14:14-16).

A New Gate,[89] Isaiah 28:5-6. The driving force that creates in us an insatiable appetite for the fast lane is our crown of pride (centering life upon the needs and presumed qualifications of self, Isaiah 28: 1). Pride gives us the unwarranted confidence (arrogance) required to build our house in the flood plain and to believe that we can control the drink. Pride causes us to be unaware that the drink can be controlling us. Thus, we don't associate our drunkenness with pride. In contrast to this picture, the reward for those depending on God is a crown

89 Old adage, "Like a calf looking at a new gate".

of glory (Isaiah 28:5).[90] This crown is associated with a gate (Isaiah 28:6). In Biblical times, all cities were protected from marauders by the city walls. It was necessary to construct gates in these walls to allow transit and commerce. The trick was how to construct the gate to allow passage to friends but not enemies. From a defense standpoint, gates were a necessary evil. The enemy knew the gates had the potential to be the weakest part of the city defenses. Therefore, the enemy would often concentrate its forces at the gate making for the necessity of turning the enemy at the gate (Isaiah 28:6).[91] Archaeology has shown that these gates were just as much about repelling as about allowing entry. Defense involved construction of side porticoes so an enemy could be spotted and attacked at a narrow aperture from corners built into the gate. The configuration of many of these gates could be likened to two capital E's facing each other. City gates were also places where city magistrates executed judgment. As we shall see from our discussion of the Cornerstone (Isaiah 28:16), this stone was laid to allow the turning of a corner. The gate, in times of siege, was the focal point between friend and enemy. The Cornerstone, when built into the gate, was the crux of the focal point, narrowing the entryway, allowing opportunity for judgment as to distinguishing friend from foe, and providing a platform for attacking foe. A picture of this is presented by Luke when

---

90 Isaiah 28:5, "In that day the Lord of Hosts", *Bayowm hahuw'*, ***The day [of the flood]...*** *yuh^{a}yeh*, ***I AM...***, *tsabaa'owt*, ***of the campaign...***, "shall be for a crown of glory" *la$^{'a}$Terot ts^{a}biy*, ***circle of beauty...***, "and for a diadem of beauty" *walitspiyrat*, Wah consecutive, ***with the circling crown...***, *tip'aaraah*, ***the beautiful ornament signifying majesty...***, "unto the residue of his people" *lish'aar 'amon*, ***to the remnant of the tribe...***

91 Isaiah 28:6, "and for a spirit of judgment" *uwlruwach*, breath, wind, ***also the intangible essence...***, *mishpaat*, ***of verdict...***, penalty, judgment in the gate, "to him that sitteth in judgment" *layowsheeb*, Qal participle active of *yawshab'* = ***him that is sitting down...***, *al-hamishpaaT*, ***in the verdict...***, "and for strength" *w^{a}hig^{a}buwraah*, Wah conjunctive of *gebuwrah* = ***in conjunction with verdict, to exercise force to attain victory...***, "to them that turn", *m^{a}shiybeey*, Hiphil [causative] participle of *shuwb* = ***causing to turn back***[away]..., "the battle", *milchaamaah*, ***the skirmish...***, combat, engagement, "to the gate", *shaa^{a}rah*, ***at the entrance***, portal...

The Cornerstone came to the gate of the city of Nain (Luke 7:12-17). At that point, the Cornerstone confronted that ancient foe of man, death, and turned him back.[92] Jesus clarified the matter when He reversed the metaphor in Matthew 16:18; He said, "And I say also unto thee, that thou art Peter, and upon this rock I will build my church; and the gates of hell shall not prevail against it."[93] The rock is the Cornerstone; the gates of hell are the entrances to the unknown. The Greek word translated as gates is *pulai* which means "to turn"[94]. The Cornerstone allows those with right-placed confidence to turn the corner beyond which there is no vision (Hades), the corner of death.

The Consumer's Report, Isaiah 28:7. Although we believe we are the consumers of the high life, in actuality, the high life is consuming us as evidenced by a glance in the mirror at "the fading flower". That glance leaves us with no confidence in the future and feeling somewhat unsettled

92 Luke 7: "12 Now when he came nigh to the gate of the city, behold, there was a dead man carried out, the only son of his mother, and she was a widow: and much people of the city was with her. 13 And when the Lord saw her, he had compassion on her, and said unto her, Weep not. 14 And he came and touched the bier: and they that bare him stood still. And he said, Young man, I say unto thee, Arise. 15 And he that was dead sat up, and began to speak. And he delivered him to his mother. 16 And there came a fear on all: and they glorified God, saying, That a great prophet is risen up among us; and, That God hath visited his people. 17 And this rumour of him went forth throughout all Judaea, and throughout all the region round about."

93 Matt 16:18 "And I say also unto thee," *kagoo de soi legoo*, And me also, as the bottom line, unto you I lay forth, "That thou art Peter", *hoti su ei petros*, because that you exist as a piece of the rock, "and upon this rock", *kai epee tautee tee petra*, and upon this, the bedrock, "I will build my church;", *oikodomeeso*, future active of *oikodomeo* = will construct the family dwelling [*oikos* = family dwelling, English, eco, *domeo* = to build, English, domestic], *mou tee ekklesian*, my called out [*ek* = out, *kaleo* = called], "and the gates of hell" *pulai*, entrance into [from *pelo* = to turn a corner, a *pen* as in *pinat*, a corner, *hadou*, no perception, [a = not, *idou* = intuitive perception], "shall not prevail against it." *Ou*, not now, not ever, *katischusousin*, future active of *katischuo* = will overpower it [*kata* = down, *ischuo* = to have force].

94 *New Testament Lexicon*, 1889, being *Grimms. Wilkes. Clavis. Novi Testamenti*, Translated and revised and enlarged by Joseph Henry Thayer, Harper & Brothers, New York, NY.

about the present. In the imagery of the hasty fruit, the eater loses self-control, becomes obsessed with the transience of the moment, the opportunity for momentary satisfaction, the fulfillment of desire. He is convinced that he has an entitlement to the fruit. He believes that he has worked hard for this moment and deserves this gratification. So he consumes the first ripe fruit he finds, it is so sweet, he gobbles another with growing lust, and then another, and another...until he has eaten too many, even some that were not ripe. Nothing is said about him harvesting some for the family or even taking any back to the house for supper. Instead, he becomes intoxicated with the moment as if the fruit were wine, as if he was "swallowed up of wine"[95] to the extent that he loses control becoming "out of the way through strong drink".[96] He develops vision problems, being unable to see things straight. He develops memory problems, forgetting that his purpose is to harvest fruit to be preserved for nourishment during the coming winter. He is viewing life in a distorted way, as through a tunnel, focused on his present enjoyment. In this manner he is able to escape the fact that the root of his problem is his preoccupation with the transience of the "high" that he is experiencing.[97] This progresses until he ends with "tables full of vomit and filthiness".[98] The lust for the transience of the moment leads him to actions that are self-destructive. Life is full of irony, the desire for something that is intrinsically good and good for us, when viewed only from the urgent perspective of the passing pleasure it can produce

---

95 Isaiah 28:7, "swallowed up of wine" *Nibl[a]uw,* Niphal [passive] imperfect of *bawlah* = ***he was in the process of being consumed by it...***

96 Isaiah 28:7, "out of the way through strong drink" *Taa'uw,* Qal perfect of *tawaw* = ***He staggers and reels, stumbling and falling down, nothing matters any more...***

97 Isaiah 28:7, "they err in vision, they stumble in judgment" *shaaguw,* Qal perfect of *shawgaw'* = ***he wanders aimlessly,*** flitting from this to that, not really going anywhere ***because of no...****baaro'eh* = ***focus, and thus he...****paaquw,* Qal perfect of *puwq* = ***is unstable having no integrity in...****p[a]liyliyaah* = ***his reasoning...***

98 Isaiah 28:8, "tables full of vomit and filthiness", ***kaalshulke, all dinner tables spread with...*** *maala'uw,* ***and replenished with...*** *qiy,* ***vomit,*** *tsoo'ah,* ***and excrement...***

for us now, ultimately is destructive. Since the promise of the fruit was a wonderful experience, it is surprising that the promise gets lost in the transcience so that, in actuality the experience becomes more than just tainted. We are left with the feeling that it is "strange how the night moves, with autumn closing in".[99]

The Hasty Fruit Syndrome, aka The (Mid)Life Crisis,[100] Isaiah 28:8. We are fascinated with personalities who take these methods to extremes. One such personality, among many, was that of Michael Jackson. His life style seems to have been configured to live the high life and stay young in order to enjoy the high life as long as possible. He was preoccupied with plastic surgery and with drugs designed to allow escape (at least in the form of sleep). He was surrounded by sycophants who provided mirrors for vanity, and company for the high life. We are interested in these futile attempts to dig in and hold onto life because each of us is preoccupied with the same kind of pursuits targeting extension of the "highs" of life and deferral of the aging process.[101] It is a striking statement about the futility of this pursuit that Michael Jackson, in spite of all his efforts, or perhaps because of them (a lifetime of paying the death tax?), died at age 50 and was buried in a lavish, gold embellished casket emblematic of the transience of possessions. Most funerals today have aspects indicative of attempts to hold onto ephemeral splendors and the resulting transient euphoria as long as possible. Perhaps this is not too different from the funerary rites of ancient peoples such as the Egyptians, Mayans, or Incas. While we think we can control the highs we seek, actually they control us even as far as the grave.

---

99 *Night Moves*, 1976, written and sung by Bob Seger and the Silver Bullet Band, album *Night Moves*.

100 "Midlife crisis", a term coined in 1965 by Elliott Jaques for "a time where adults come to realize their own mortality and how much time is left in their life." http://en.wikipedia.org

101 *The Michael Jackson Tapes*, Rabbi Shmuley Boteach, quoted in *Spiritual Adviser's Book Searches Jackson's Soul*, September 27, 2009, Victor Epstein, the *San Antonio Express-News*.

Oblivious, Isaiah 28:9-13[102]

"None so blind as those that will not see."
Commentary on the Whole Bible, 1708, Mathew Henry.

Ripe for the Picking, Isaiah 28:9-12. The produce of the Hasty Fruit Syndrome, therefore, is achieved in the eater of the fruit. It is not only the fruit that ripens, but, strange as it may seem, the eater also ripens. The process of increasing obsession with the temporal desire afforded by the ripe fruit is ironically accompanied by a ripening of the eater.[103] Ripeness is aptly depicted "as them that are weaned". It is the calf (the consumer) that ripens toward weaning, not the milk (that consumed) or the dam (source of that consumed). This picture also vividly portrays the vulnerability associated with ripening. The "picking" of a ripe calf at weaning causes considerable stress to the calf (he loses the nurture and nutrients provided by his mama), causing this to be the most vulnerable time in the calf's life. This vulnerability comes at a surprising time in the calf's life when he should be full of vim, vigor, and vitality. The day before the calf is weaned, he is content with life in the pasture with mama; he does not suspect what is in store for him. For us, it only takes a few tricks with the mind to achieve a comfortable complacence that, regardless of the evidence in the mirror, the present "status quo" (pre-weaned status) is permanent. The process of eating the fruit causes the eater to suffer the illusion that he has "arrived" (ripened)

---

102 Isaiah 28: "9 Whom shall he teach knowledge? and whom shall he make to understand doctrine? them that are weaned from the milk, and drawn from the breasts. 10 For precept must be upon precept, precept upon precept; line upon line, line upon line; here a little, and there a little: 11 For with stammering lips and another tongue will he speak to this people. 12 To whom he said, This is the rest wherewith ye may cause the weary to rest; and this is the refreshing: yet they would not hear. 13 But the word of the LORD was unto them precept upon precept, precept upon precept; line upon line, line upon line; here a little, and there a little; that they might go, and fall backward, and be broken, and snared, and taken."

103 Isaiah 28:9 "them that are weaned from the milk and drawn from the breasts", weaned translates *g^amuwlee*, Qal participle passive of *gawmul* = ***him that is becoming mature, moving on from the milk,*** the process results in a ripening such as takes place when a cow weans her calf [to toil, repay, deal out to]...

in that he has learned everything he needs to know. If this thought pattern becomes endemic in the population as it did in Israel *circa* 700 B.C.E. (and as it has in every generation before or since), then the appropriate, if rhetorical, question is: who is teachable?[104] Every attempt at teaching is lost on those who are buffered in their complacent status and are totally "consumed" with themselves. They are only in tune with their desires for immediate satisfaction. It seems to them a happy coincidence that this opportunity for satisfaction (taking advantage of opportune pleasure) is accomplished in the same event as their perceived opportunity to escape a pressing, unpleasant reality. The reality urgently requiring escape is that they can't realistically hold on to anything indefinitely. So, focused on themselves, they take the opportunity to license (and lose) themselves to self-indulgence. They do this under the guise of the extenuating circumstance of perceived transient opportunity for delight. These "ripe" ones view any teaching as coming from one with "stammering lips and another tongue".[105] A method many employ to escape coming to terms with their mortality is through directing their attention to an all-consuming distraction forcing the issue into their subconscious. Distractions (Hasty Fruit) can come in many flavors. One possibility is to become occupied in a captivating activity. Such are workaholics who narrow their focus only to losing themselves in accomplishing a job and then in weariness.[106]

Lost, Isaiah 28:13. These "ripe" ones go into deep cover by disengaging from reality. This is a natural consequence of their goal to avoid the

---

104 Isaiah 28:9 "whom shall he teach knowledge?" *miy yowree*: Qal [active] imperfect of yawrah = ***to whom does he [God] have the opportunity of informing?*** *Yaabiyn*, Hiphil imperfect of *biyn* = ***and where is the window of opportunity for discernment?***

105 Isaiah 28:11, "stammering lips and another tongue" *la^a^geey* = ***[He will seem as] a foreigner speaking unintelligibly...***

106 The author of Isaiah may be referring to this method of self-distraction in Isaiah 28:12, "to whom he said" *'aamar*, Qal [active] perfect of *awmar* = ***he [God] explained fully...*** "this is the rest", *menuwchaw* = ***this is to be at home...*** [feminine for *nooakh* = to settle in, be comfortable] "wherewith ye may cause", *haaniychuw* = masculine, ***where one can go free into an open space, something needed by...***"the weary", *lee'aayeep* = ***those languishing, fainting as if weaned and thus deprived of nourishment, exhausted, in need of...***

association between their activity and their covenant with their mortality. They, therefore, do not possess the desire to explore the truth. Nor do they have the ability to focus on any teaching. This lack of focus we call attention deficit disorder. This disorder can be the consequence of twin drives: the drive to satisfy the desire of the moment while, at the same time, hide from the motive for the desire. It is difficult, for example, to focus on God or on algebra, for that matter, when all one can think about is (the transience of) sex. The "ripe ones" so focused on escape as to "drown their sorrows" in some activity or some drug, become "burned out" and weary because of a dearth of inspiration.[107] Those so affected are irritated with the word that has the potential of becoming their inspiration, thinking of it as just a bunch of restricting, if not rhetorical rules.[108] The result of avoiding the truth of the covenant made with death is that the cost of the death tax escalates causing their lives to lose focus, purpose and meaning. Thus, they wander about and stumble around in the dark, ultimately losing control of their journey. [109] I have acted out my Covenant with Death by jogging. I have worked on the supposition

107 Isaiah 28:12, "to rest and this is the refreshing", *hamargeehaa* = to twinkle, be disturbed of mind as if by ***inspiration...***"yet they would not hear" *sh^a^mowa* = Qal perfect of *shawmah* = ***and thus they could not pay attention...***

108 Isaiah 28:13, "the word of the Lord was upon them", *d^a^bar* = ***The cause, case of business of YHWH...*** *w^a^haayaah,* Wah conjunctive [showing relation to the previous statement] Qal perfect of *hawyaw*= ***in conjunction with their failure to listen, His cause has become as stable as...***"precept upon precept", *Tsawlaatsaaw* = ***commandment compounded with commandment that can be avoided only if one can maintain some distraction...***"here a little, there a little" (*shaam zaeer* = ***and if the distraction can be maintained, it [His cause] seems as dwindling insufficiency...,*** like twiddle dee, twiddle dum...

109 Isaiah 28:13, "that they may go", *yeel^a^kuw* = Qal [active] perfect of *yawlak* = ***[allowing them to make] an active departure from the journey...***"fall backward:", *w^a^kaashluwaachowr,* Wah conjunctive Qal [active] perfect of *kawshal'* = ***in conjunction with that detour, actively stumbling and falling on their backside...*** "and be broken" *w^a^nisbaaruw,* Wah conjunctive Niphal [passive] perfect of *shawbar'* = ***in turn, being broken up...***"snared" *w^a^nowq^a^shuw,* Wah conjunctive Niphal (passive) perfect of *yawkoshe* = ***and thus attracted by the [diversionary] bait, and entrapped...***"taken" *w^a^nolkaaduw,* Wah conjunctive Niphal [passive] perfect of *lawkad* = ***resulting in being*** captured, imprisoned, frozen, ***possessed [making no progress in life's journey]...***

that if I jog every day, there is proof that I am still healthy so I won't die on that day (unless I am run over by a truck or get lost or mugged by murdering thugs). Jogging is also appealing to me in that it provides adequate rhythm and monotony that combines with the endorphin release required to cause me to "lose" myself. Several years ago I visited for the first time Bloemfontein, South Africa, an Afrikaans-speaking city of 370,000 people. I was to be the after dinner speaker at a cattle meeting at 7:30 p.m. on the day of our arrival. We traveled all day, finally checking into our Bed and Breakfast at 5:00 p.m. I changed into jogging attire, took my room key, and hastened to get in a quick run. My plan was to go out 18 minutes and return by the same route to the B&B so that I could give my speech at the appointed time. I executed my plan like clockwork, "losing" myself in the run: the only problem being that when I returned, I was not at the B&B. Magically, everything had changed: the sun had set, it was dark, a sudden storm had blown up, it was raining and lightning, instead of a B&B, there was a grocery store. After an adequate period of dithering, I bit my lip, went into the store to admit my predicament and ask for help. As I was going in, I met a woman who was coming out. I muttered something about jogging and being lost. She said, in English (I don't speak Afrikaans), "Look on your key for the B&B address, and I will take you there". What a concept, to find a wise person willing to help a complete stranger on a dark and fearful night. It was a good plan, too. But...nothing was on that key except an electronic remote opener for the security gate. For the first time, I wondered why they needed a security gate. So, as she drove me down dark streets, I pointed the remote gate opener out the window, clicking on gates that looked "right" until, glory be, one of them opened. When I finally delivered my speech that night, I was forced to explain why I was late. I had to admit that, on my own, I not only "lost" myself running, I had become hopelessly lost, and if that woman had not had mercy on me, I would have been in deep trouble. I was ripe for the picking, having disengaged myself from reality and being in need of a good guide to extract me from my lost condition.

PART 2

The Repeal of the Death Tax: Ruling the Edge

"End? No, the journey doesn't end here. Death is just another path... One that we all must take. The grey rain-curtain of this world rolls back, and all change to silver glass. White shores... and beyond, a far green country under a swift sunrise."

Gandalf, *The Return of the King, The Lord of the Rings*, 1955, J.R.R. Tolkien.

CHAPTER 3

BREAKING THE COVENANT WITH DEATH: LOOKING BEYOND THE EDGE

Silent as the Grave, Isaiah 28:14-16, Romans 9:33[110]

"I'm dying to be alive, yeah
Not trying to just survive, yeah-yeah
Let's not go through our lives
Without just dying to be alive"

Dying to Be Alive, 2000, , written and sung by Zachary Walker Hanson, Isaac Hanson, Taylor Hanson, album, *This Time Around*

The Flag Stone, Isaiah 28:14-15a. Now we come to the "flag" passage of Isaiah explicitly referred to by Paul in Romans 9:33 and 10:11. These two verses bracket Paul's *remez*, his amplification of Isaiah 28. In these

110 Romans 9: "33 As it is written, Behold, I lay in Sion a stumblingstone and rock of offence: and whosoever believeth on him shall not be ashamed." Isaiah28: "14 Wherefore hear the word of the LORD, ye scornful men, that rule this people which is in Jerusalem. 15 Because ye have said, We have made a Covenant with Death, and with hell are we at agreement; when the overflowing scourge shall pass through, it shall not come unto us: for we have made lies our refuge, and under falsehood have we hid ourselves: 16 Therefore thus saith the Lord GOD, Behold, I lay in Zion for a foundation, a stone, a tried stone, a precious Cornerstone, a sure foundation: he that believeth shall not make haste."

intervening verses he describes the only possible way out of our Covenant with Death. Paul assumes that we know that Isaiah wrote that our only hope of escape from our oppressive, yet self-imposed death tax is to "hear the word of the Lord".[111] Perhaps if Paul had not focused our attention on Isaiah 28, we would have thought that this admonishment to "hear" could have been narrowly meant for only "men that rule this people" (Isaiah 28:14) in the limited context of the immediate problem Judah had with Assyria *circa* 700 B.C.E.[112] But, because of Paul's focus on Isaiah 28, we realize Isaiah had two audiences in mind: the narrow one of Judah who was contemplating a covenant with Assyria or Egypt and a broader set of "scornful men" that includes all who have a "hasty fruit problem". It is to this broader audience that Isaiah speaks when he says..."Because ye have said, We have made a Covenant with Death, and with hell are we at agreement; when the overflowing scourge shall pass through, it shall not come unto us" (Isaiah 28:15). Because of something we said, we forced the Lord to take action.[113] What we said (to the Lord, or at least to ourselves) was, "Don't worry about us; we have made our own private deal with mortality." Our big problem that concerns God is that we have made our own private agreement with death, circumventing Him. This is what provoked the Lord to act.[114]

---

111 Isaiah 28:14, "hear the word of the Lord", *shim'uw* = Qal imperative of *shawmah'* = ***[To escape this wasting away syndrome] you must pay attention, listen...to what the Lord says...***[in vs. 15]

112 Isaiah 28:14. "ye scornful men," *'ansheey*, **mortals**, *laatsown*, ***who are derisive*** [*luwts*, to make a mouth, to scoff], "that rule this people which is in Jerusalem", *mush^{a}leey*, Qal participle active of *mawshal'* = ***having dominion***/authority ***over***, *haa'aam haze hasher bi-y^{a}ruwshaalaaim*, ***this tribe which is in the city of peace...***

113 Isaiah 28:15, "Because ye have said", *^{a}martem*, Qal perfect of *awmar*, ***[the wasting away syndrome was the fruit of what we said, and] we said it like we meant it, perhaps trying to convince ourselves of its truth, what we said [to the Lord was]...***

114 Isaiah 28:15. "We have made a Covenant with Death", *kaaratnuw b^{a}rit*, Qal perfect of kawrath = ***we cut a cutting, signing it with blood in a compact with...*** *etmaawet*, ***the dead,*** possibly poor covenant partners unlikely to carry out their end of the deal... "and with hell" *w^{a}im sh^{a}owl* = ***and with the place of the dead, hades...*** "are we in agreement" *'aasiynuw*, Qal perfect of *awsaw'* = ***look what we have accomplished, we have solved our problem with mortality***; *chozeh'*, ***It is our compact for the future, our vision...***

The Cryptic Crypt,[115] Isaiah 28:15. We are forced to admit that sources of information about the other side of the grave are limited. Scientists can only gain knowledge about an issue by making hypotheses and collecting data to either substantiate or refute the hypotheses. Numerous hypotheses exist about death and "the great beyond", but there is no reliable data. This necessitates that we "hear the word of the LORD". Part of Isaiah's stated reason for the imperative requiring us to listen is that "with hell we are in agreement". The Hebrew word translated as hell is *Sh^{a}owl*[116] which is the place of no return, corresponding to the black holes of the universe, a place emitting no information. The Septuagint translates this word as *Hades* (Greek for no intuitive perception). Not only are we lacking physical data about what is beyond the Edge, but we don't even have a basis for an intuitive guess (hypothesis). The New Testament[117] has three Greek words translated as hell, but they all relate to darkness emphasizing the difficulty in seeing beyond the grave.[118] Of particular interest is the word

115 Cryptic: hidden, concealed, secret, mysterious, [Greek, *kruptos*]. Crypt: an underground vault [Greek, *kruptos*, hidden]. *The American Heritage Dictionary of the English Language*, 1969, William Morris, Ed., American Heritage Publishing Co., Boston, and Houghton Mifflin Co., New York, NY, ISBN 395-09064-4.

116 Transliterated to Sheol in Amplified and ASV.

117 *Interlinear Transliterated Bible*, Copyright © 1994, 2003 by Biblesoft, Inc.; *Novum Testamentum Graece Nestle-Aland 27th Ed.* © 1898 and 1993 by Deutsche Bibelgesellschaft, Stuttgart; PCSB Greek and PCSB Hebrew fonts, Copyright © 1992, Galaxie Software, Garland, TX.

118 *Sh^{a}owl* [from *shawal* = to inquire, to ask "How are you?", to consult, the proper name, Saul] is the only word translated as hell in the Old Testament, the Septuagint translates *Sh^{a}owl* as *Hades* [*a* = no, *eidos* = intuitive perception], and this word is translated as hell in the New Testament in Matthew 11:43, 16:18, Luke 10:15; 16:23; Acts 2:27,31; Revelation 1:18; 6:8; 20:13,14. *Gehenna* [*ge* = gorge, gully, *Hinnom* = proper name in Isaiah 66:24; Jeremiah 2:23; 7:29-33; 18:2; 19:2; Micah 1:5; Zechariah 11:13] is translated as hell in Matthew 5:22,29,30; 10:28; 18:9; 23:15,32; Mark 9:43,45,47; Luke 12:5; James 3:6. The other Greek word translated as hell in the New Testament is in 2 Peter 2:4 "cast them down to hell", *tartaroosas* from *tartarus*, the dark abyss in reference to the inability to see it for the lack of light. *Young's Analytical Concordance to the Bible*, 1975, Robert Young, William B. Eerdmans Publishing Co., Grand Rapids, MI, ISBN 0-8028-2283-5.

Gehenna, which refers to the valley of Hinnom that separated the hill of Zion from the "hill of evil council".[119] It was in this valley that unspeakable acts were performed in attempts to know the unknowable, the other side of the grave.[120] The insatiable curiosity and drive to know the other side of the grave assumes that God has not satisfactorily taken care of the matter. This curiosity embodies our agreement with hell and is reflected in our generation with the fixation on such topics as zombies, vampires, witches, wizards, Halloween, the Day of the Dead, *etc.* The etiological root of the word *Sh*^{a}*owl* carries the force of the mystery of the silence of the grave. That root means to inquire, especially to ask, "How are you?" The fundamental question left for us about the grave is embodied in the word, "Hello?" The temptation is to stand before the tomb and ask, "Hello, is anyone in there?" The fear, since no answer ever comes, is that the answer is "no". We can become obsessed with the process of exploring this question. Because we cannot discover the answer (having no basis for either hypothesis or data collection), we make up fantastic stories in attempts to satiate our hunger to know. The "agreement with hell" amounts to our insatiable and therefore futile occupation with mortality embodying the death tax. Because we are in this "agreement with hell", God was forced to act.

---

119 "The hill of evil council" referred to our agreement with hell, our insatiable and unsettling curiosity about death and the great beyond , the hill of Zion points toward God and His Rock and thus to God's response to our agreement with hell, the Cornerstone. *The New Brown, Driver, Briggs, Gesenius Hebrew and English Lexicon,* 1979, Francis Brown, S.R. Driver, Charles A. Briggs, Hendrickson Publishers, Peabody, MA, ISBN 0-913573-20-5.

120 2 Chronicles 33:6 "And he [Manasseh, *Menasheh* = causing to forget, vs. 1] caused his children to pass through the fire in the valley of the son of Hinnom: also he observed times," *w*^{a}*owneen,* Wah conjunctive Piel perfect of *'anan* = and acted covertly, clouding over, "and used enchantments," *w*^{a}*nicheesh,* Wah conjunctive Piel perfect of *nachash'* = and whispered prognostications, "and used witchcraft," *w*^{a}*kisheep,* Wah conjunctive of *kashap'* = and whispered a spell, "and dealt with a familiar spirit," *w*^{a}*aasaas,* Wah conjunctive Qal perfect of *awsaw'* = and accomplished *owb* = necromancy, and consulted with the dead [troubled spirits] "and with wizards:" *w*^{a}*yidowniy,* Wah conjunctive of *yidoniy* = and conjured ghosts, "he wrought much evil" *la*^{a}*sowt,* Qal infinitive construct of *awsaw'* = appointed… *hirdaah,* Hiphil perfect of *rawsaw'* = authorized… *haara'* = adversity, calamity, "in the sight of the LORD, to provoke him to anger."

White Lies, A Place to Hide, Isaiah 28:15b. But, it is our story and we are sticking to it: we knew there was a problem with life from the beginning. We knew the problem was that someday our lives will cease and the cessation will be a very personal event. We circumvented this eventuality by telling ourselves that although others will succumb to disease, we will not. And, if we do become diseased, we will be able to beat it. Our doctors will be better than the doctors of others suffering from the malady; we will drink five gallons of carrot juice every day and drown the disease in carrot juice.[121] We cannot afford to acknowledge, even to ourselves, that we have made this compact. Acknowledgement negates the whole reason for the compact: so that we can live our lives free of the cloud of the impending doom of our inevitable demise/defeat.[122] We have sold ourselves the lie that when death arrives, we won't be there to accept it, and death will be forced just to pass us by. It will come to others, but we can avoid it, at least for today, and that is all that matters. If we don't die today, we will never die, right? We know this is not quite right, and it doesn't sound very good when we enunciate it, but we don't have to enunciate it. It will be our little secret, okay? You might say we are too smart to sell ourselves on this kind of lie; we have more brains than that. But, what about the many people who build their houses on the coast to enjoy the sun and surf; how do they rationalize the periodic hurricanes? The people rebuilding their beach houses along the American gulf coast after hurricane Rita or Ike: what was their rationale? Are they so different from us? It is only natural for us to rationalize our mortality; if we don't we will never have any fun. We will worry ourselves to an

---

121 Isaiah 28:15, "when the overflowing scourge shall pass through" *showTeep*, Qal participle active of *shawtaf'* = ***the inundating...*** *showt,* ***lash whip as the sea...*** *ya^a^kob*, Qal [active] imperfect of *awbar'* = ***will rise and begin to cover over...*** "it shall not come unto us." lo' *yabow'eenuw*, Qal [active] imperfect of *bow* = ***but it will not run us down...*** "For we have made lies our refuge" *samnuw'*, Qal [active] perfect of *suwm* = ***we have committed ourselves to...****kaazaab*, ***[self] deception...*** *machceenuw*, ***as our shelter, our protection from danger...***

122 Isaiah 28:15 "and under falsehood have we hid ourselves" *uwbasheqer* = ***with a sham-fraud...*** [from *shawkar* = to cheat, be untrue {to yourself}] *nictaar^a^nuw* = Niphal [passive] imperfect of *sawthar* = ***we have been keeping it secret,*** it has been concealed. God's response to our little secret is in Isaiah 28:16...

early grave; is that not ironic? But, where can we hide except in some rationalization we fabricate? For our own good, we must give our weary minds some avenue to escape. Otherwise, the ever-present gloom that unavoidably accompanies our mortal condition will drag us down. We are afraid no one can help us in our urgent need to settle our fevered minds about the mortality problem. We become desperate to solve the problem ourselves. This is our story and we are sticking to it.

Illustration 3, Rites of Passage. Cemeteries all over the world are full of rocks, such as this 5,000 year old Irish "passage tomb" (upper left), the Jewish cemetery across the Kidron Valley from The Dome of The Rock in Jerusalem (upper right), the rock that temporarily held "The Rock" (Gordon's Tomb, Jerusalem, lower left), and the one in Graham, Texas where the author's grandfather (and namesake) and grandmother are buried (lower right).

A Sign of the Times, All Times, Isaiah 28:16. Since this book is exposing scripture in contexts, it is necessary to discuss "the rock" both in the context of Romans 9-10 and in that of Isaiah 28. As these scriptures are exposed, I will show different aspects of the metaphor, but there will necessarily be some repetition. Because we feel that we must make some kind of private deal with our mortality, God was forced to act. His action is spelled out in Isaiah 28:16. The spelling begins with an exclamation of surprise: "Behold".[123] It is a surprise that God understood our plight so intimately that He made response even before most people experienced the problem. What He did about our plight is also a surprise. Since God's ways are above our ways,[124] we cannot at first blush understand His response.

Rites of Passage, Isaiah 28:16a. Our failure to comprehend God's ways may be why Isaiah presents God's action in our behalf in terms of our common experience, a rock. We have all experienced a rock; we have a common understanding of the qualities of rocks: igneous, sedimentary, and the like. Most peoples who have inhabited the earth have associated rock with death. Cemeteries all over the world are full of rocks. Ancient arrangements of rocks such as Stonehenge have been associated with funerary rites.[125] Other ancient rock edifices found in many parts of the world such as the ziggurats of Mesopotamia, the pyramids of Egypt, Mexico, Peru, Japan and China, and the Passage Tombs of Ireland, Scotland, Spain, and Israel are commonly thought to have been meant to be portals between this life and the next. Even in movies such as *2001, A Space Odyssey* and *Harry Potter, the Deathly Hallows Part II*, rocks are associated with the transcendence of man. Isaiah builds on this common experiential understanding with statements foreign to us, expanding our experience base and giving us a common platform for understanding God's response to our dilemma with our mortality. His response is in

123 Isaiah 28:16. "Behold", *hinnay*, ***Pay attention for I am going to tell you a surprising thing that is not intuitively obvious and is outside of your frame of reference...***

124 Ecclesiastes 11:5 "God's ways are as hard to discern as the pathways of the wind." NLT

125 "Researchers find 'Bluehenge'" by Gregory Katz, Associated Press, in the *San Antonio Express-News*, October 7, 2009.

terms of a particular rock. Isaiah begins by saying that this particular rock wasn't always "there", but God had to put it "there".[126] We commonly think of rocks as being formed as a part of ancient geological processes. The only rocks we think of as being placed are rocks like mile markers and building stones that are placed by man for a purpose. It doesn't occur to us that God may also have placed a rock for a purpose. But, according to Isaiah 28, God did place a rock, and He did place it for a purpose.

May God Bless Texas,[127] Isaiah 28:16a. The purpose of the Rock is closely associated with the location of placement. The question arises as to why "there" had to be Zion; why couldn't somewhere in Texas do just as well? If "there" could have been Texas, it would have done wonders for the tourist industry. The distinguishing characteristic about Mount Zion, the location of the Jewish Temple and the Islamic *es-Sakhra* (Arabic for the rock),[128] the Dome of the Rock, is not that it is a conspicuous or beautiful mountain. It is a hill, not even the tallest, or the most conspicuous hill in the vicinity. It has no inherent beauty to write home about. So, what makes this hill prominent? As the name of the Dome indicates, it is this particular rock that sets it apart, making it of singular importance.

The Rock That Is Higher Than I, Isaiah 28:16, Romans 9:33

"Oh! sometimes the shadows are deep,
And rough seems the path to the goal,
And sorrows, sometimes how they sweep
Like tempests down over the soul.
O then to the Rock let me fly
To the Rock that is higher than I"

126 Isaiah 28:16, "I lay" *yoceed*, Piel (active) perfect of *yawsad'* = ***I fixed firm***, appointed, ordained, built into the foundation ***as an already accomplished fact...***

127 *God Blessed Texas*, 1993, sung by Little Texas, album *Big Time*, written by Porter Howell and Brady Seals.

128 The *Al-Aqsa* Mosque *circa* A.D. 709-715.

The Rock That is Higher Than I, 1871, written by Erastus Johnson during the American financial panic of 1871, music by William Johnson.

The Rock of our Salvation, Isaiah 28:16a. Isaiah systematically characterizes the rock through careful selection of words that build upon each other, finally presenting a composite picture of the nature of the rock:

Signal Rock. First, he calls it a "foundation" translating a Hebrew word meaning the rock had an appointment.[129] Since the rock was laid in Zion (*B^{a}tsiyown*),[130] its appointment was to be a waymarker, a sign showing the way, keeping the traveler on course, keeping him from getting lost.

Milestone. Second, he calls it a "stone", translating a Hebrew word meaning that the rock not only is appointed for the purpose of being a waymarker, but it also has the potential to accomplish that purpose.[131] The rock can be useful: it can be built upon as masonry because it is solid. As such, it can serve as a marker for all men for all time. If the rock had been flawed, had soft spots, it would not be dependable as masonry. One could not have confidence in using such a rock for any purpose requiring stability or durability; its potential would have been limited.

Touchstone. Third, he calls it a "tried stone" meaning it had been assayed as to usefulness. The stone was scrutinized (by the traveler) and found

---

129 Isaiah 28:16 "foundation", *yoceed*, Piel imperfect of *yawcad'* = ***settle in for a consultation, process of appointment...***

130 Isaiah 28:16, "in Zion" *b^{a}tsiyown*, ***in Zion as a permanent, prominent, conspicuous monument, a signal...*** As discussed earlier, the Hebrew root, *tseeyone* = ***guiding monument***, waymark, a signal as a mile marker, conspicuous prominence, the place where God provided a ram to free Isaac from the sacrifice required by God of Abraham (Genesis 22:13).

131 Isaiah 28:16 "a stone" *'aaben*, masonry from *bawnaw'* = [having the character required] for building, construction, raw material, having utility, ***useful [for building or other purposes]...***

to be authentic (at least by the traveler depicted in Isaiah 28). It was proven to be all that it was advertised to be. Some stones (waymarkers) along roads in ancient times were "counterfeit"; they were laid along the path by want-to-be robbers who meant to mislead travelers, causing them to leave the populous road, leading them onto more desolate paths, making them vulnerable to the robber's malicious intent. As we have seen in Isaiah 8, not everyone found the stone to be useful; some found it to be a stumblingstone. It may seem odd that the examination process not only characterized the stone, but also characterized the examiner. The assay of the stone proved that it, in turn, is useful as a tool for assaying.[132] Through the assaying process, both the stone and the assayer were revealed as to their true value and usefulness. This is true because the characterization of the stone is dependent on the nature of the value system of the assayer. The nature of the value system is a reflection on the character of the evaluator. In ancient times certain stones were used to assay the purity of various metals. An examination of the stone was required to determine if it had the character required for this use. Stones were also used in the process of examining people. Ancients felt that the process of torture could determine the true nature of the victim. The common method of torture was to begin by inflicting mild levels of pain, thereafter incrementally increasing the level, but concurrently providing a readily available "way out" for the victim. All the victim had to do to stop the ever-increasing infliction of pain was to reach out and touch a stone placed in easy reach of the victim. When the victim had "reached the end of his rope" he could touch the stone, confess, and the torture would cease. It was felt that all people live "under cover" but each has a

132 Isaiah 28:16 "a tried stone", *bokhan*, tested and approved, ***examined to be*** bona fide, ***authentic [proven to be as it appeared: useful]***, from *bawkhan'* = scrutinized, tortured, allowed to vindicate itself, given due process...

breaking point; the point at which they give up their "cover" and reveal their true nature. This point is signified by touching the stone.[133]

Gemstone. Fourth, he calls it a "precious stone".[134] Although, in rocky terrain, rocks can become mundane: many having seemingly no purpose. This rock, however, is of consequence to the traveler. It has utility, enabling him to accomplish some aspect of his journey and in the process providing the traveler with a self-portrait, a snapshot of himself. As in the case of some polished gemstones, one can see a reflection of himself by looking into the stone.[135] Such a rock is valuable.

Tombstone. Fifth, he calls it a "cornerstone".[136] What this particular milestone allows the traveler to accomplish is that it shows the traveler

---

133 Luke 16: "19 There was a certain rich man, which was clothed in purple and fine linen, and fared sumptuously every day: 20 And there was a certain beggar named Lazarus, which was laid at his gate, full of sores, 21 And desiring to be fed with the crumbs which fell from the rich man's table: moreover the dogs came and licked his sores. 22 And it came to pass, that the beggar died, and was carried by the angels into Abraham's bosom: the rich man also died, and was buried; 23 And in hell he lift up his eyes, being in torments, and seeth Abraham afar off, and Lazarus in his bosom. 24 And he cried and said, Father Abraham, have mercy on me, and send Lazarus, that he may dip the tip of his finger in water, and cool my tongue; for I am tormented in this flame. 25 But Abraham said, Son, remember that thou in thy lifetime receivedst thy good things, and likewise Lazarus evil things: but now he is comforted, and thou art tormented. 26 And beside all this, between us and you there is a great gulf fixed: so that they which would pass from hence to you cannot; neither can they pass to us, that would come from thence." In Luke 16:23, the word "torments" translates *basanos*, the touchstone, from *basis* = a walk (down to the bottom) English: basement, basal, bass, basset, to come to the end of one's rope, the point at which one can no longer maintain his "cover" but reveals his basic insecurities. Called *basanite* or in Latin, *lapis Lydius* which was a stone used to assay metal bearing rock as to its purity. This kind of torment has a purpose. The purpose is not punishment; it is a matter of becoming honest (with oneself/God). The one being tormented/tortured will confess, show who he is.

134 Isaiah 28:16 "precious stone" *yiqaat*, valuable, rare, prized, ***consequential...***

135 http://www.mirrorhistory.com

136 Isaiah 28:16 "cornerstone" *pinat*, pinnacle, angle, from *pen* = ***[allowing the traveler to] turn (a corner)***, verb *panah'* = to turn to face [the enemy]...

that the road is turning a corner. In light of the context of Isaiah 28, the corner is the corner of death. We cannot see around this corner. The Cornerstone provides the opportunity for the traveler to turn the corner of death, allowing him to travel beyond his line of sight. If it wasn't for the Cornerstone, we might think that the road makes a dead end, with the emphasis on dead. But, if we take heed of the Cornerstone, we can "turn the corner" and follow the road on the other side of the (tomb)stone. For the traveler to continue toward his destination, it is imperative for him to pay attention to the Cornerstone.

Bedrock.[137] Sixth, he calls it a "sure foundation". The Cornerstone is solidly connected to the earth, tying the earth together into one holistic mass. In the same way, it also connects man's total journey to make it "whole". If the traveler somehow misses the Cornerstone, the whole journey is for naught.[138] The traveler will "lose his way", possibly wandering until something dire happens. The purpose of the journey is

---

137 "Bedrock: the solid rock that underlies all soil, the lowest or bottom level, a fundamental principle", *The American Heritage Dictionary of the English Language*, 1969, William Morris, Ed., American Heritage Publishing Co., Boston, MA, ISBN 395-09064-4.

138 John 3:16 "For God so loved the world", *houtos gar* (the reason [for the possibility of self-perpetuating life] being..., *agapeesan*, aorist indicative active of *agapao* = much taken with [from *agan* = much], *ho Theos*, [is] the God, *ton kosmon*, [to] the cosmos, the orderly arrangement [from *komizo* = that tended to] "that he gave his only begotten Son,", *hooste ton Huion*, it follows that the Son, *ton monogenee*, the only one generated, *edooken*, aorist indicative active of didomai = He, no doubt, at one time gave, "that whosoever believeth in him" *hina*, so that, *pas ho*, each and every one, *pisteuoon*, present active participle of *pisteuo* = who continually is having confidence, *eis auton*, into Him, "should not perish,", *mee*, might not, *apoleetai*, aorist subjunctive passive of *apollumi* = possibly be fully destroyed [*apo*=off, *olethros* = ruined], "but have everlasting life." *all'* the [only other] alternative [to being fully destroyed], *echee*, present subjunctive active of *echo* = [is that he] might hold onto, *zooeen*, zest, *aioonion*, [self-]perpetuating [from *aion* = into the age].

to arrive at the destination. Unless the traveler heeds the message of the Cornerstone, the journey will be a failure.[139]

The Prince of Peace, Isaiah 28:16. In summary, it is the foundation stone for abundant living rooted in the strong tradition of Abraham.[140] The location of the stone (Zion) had a strong tradition even before Abraham arrived at the spot. The origin of the worship of Jehovah at this place fades into the misty past, pre-Israel, pre-history. It is first brought to our attention in Genesis 14:18 with the introduction of the "king of Salem" (literally, the prince of peace),[141] Melchizedek, whose name meant the king of righteousness.[142] Melchizedek comes to our attention out of nowhere, his linage and roots are not explained. It is like he, or his kind, existed primordially. The tradition of being at peace by being right, and being right by sacrifice, extends back in time as far as anyone can remember. It extends back in time even for cultures that, as far as we know, have histories independent of the "Salem Tradition" such as the Aztec of Mexico. Thus, a foundation

139 Isaiah 28:16, It is a "sure foundation", *muwcaad' muwcaad'* repeated for emphasis: ***the foundation is solid, solid,*** from *yawcad* = to sit down together, to commune, take council, as succinctly stated in the song, *How Firm a Foundation*, 1787, John Keith: "The soul that on Jesus doth lean for repose, I will not, I will not, desert to his foes; That soul, though all hell should endeavor to shake, I'll never, no never, no never forsake."

140 Isaiah 28:16, To put it all together: it is "a foundation stone", *aaben*, ***a stone that can be built upon,*** "a tried stone," *bochan*, **one examined to be true,** "a precious Cornerstone" *pinat*, ***the crucial, signal pinnacle that is...****yiqrat*, ***rare, one of a kind...*** "a sure foundation" *moosawd' moosawd'*, ***that is settled, settled...***

141 Joshua 10:1 "Adoni-zedek king of Jerusalem" *Adoniy-Tsedek*, Lord of rightness [similar to "Melchizedek"], *melek*, king of...*Yerushalaim* can have the root, *y^aruw* = a founding...*Salem* = of peace, *Commentary on the Old Testament*, 1866-1891, C.F. Kiel and F. Delitzsch, T&T Clark, Edinburgh, updated 1996, Hendrickson Publishers Inc., Peabody, Massachusetts.

142 Genesis 14:18, "And Melchizedek", *Uw-Malkiy-Tsedeq*, king of rightness, "king of Salem" *melek*, king, royalty, of...*Salem*, of peace, "brought forth bread and wine: and he was the priest of the most high God" *koheen*, mediator, *l^aeEl*, of The Almighty, *elyown*, who is above it all.

principle is that being at peace is rooted in coming to grips with death and that sacrifice is required for us to come to grips with death. The Jewish temple and the Islamic Dome were built on this rock because it was here that the patriarch Abraham had a close encounter with his Maker. Here, Abraham demonstrated his confidence in God by attempting to accomplish God's requirement of him. God required the elderly Abraham (providentially and ironically named, the father of many) to sacrifice his only (legitimate?)[143] son Isaac.[144]

Solid as a Rock,[145] Isaiah 28:16. This mysterious place was also called Jehovah-Jirah or Moriah.[146] It was at Moriah that God provided the ram as a sacrifice substitute for Isaac after Abraham had demonstrated

143 But, what about Ishmael? Gen 16:15 "And Hagar bare Abram a son: and Abram called his son's name, which Hagar bare, Ishmael", *Yishma'el*, = God will hear. Genesis 17:5 "thy name shall be Abraham; for a father of many nations have I made thee", *Abrawhawm 'ab h^{a}mown*, the father of many a father of many, purposefully redundant for emphasis.

144 Gen 17:19 "And God said, Sarah thy wife shall bear thee a son indeed; and thou shalt call his name Isaac" *Yitschaaq*, laughter, mockery [from *tsachaaq* = to sport, laugh [in derision, scorn}Princess Sarah [*Saaraah*, nobility {*sar* = chief, having dominion} laughed when she was told that she would bear a child {Genesis 18:12}].

145 *Solid (as a Rock)*, 1984, Nickolas Ashford and Valerie Simpson, album *Solid*.

146 Genesis 22:14, "the Jehovah-jirah": *YHWH-yirah*, God will see to it, or God will appear, otherwise called Moriah in Genesis 22:2: *Mowriyah*, which could have three roots: 1) *yereh* = teach or the land of the teaching, 2) *yerah* = fear or the land of the worship/reverence, or 3) *ra'ah* = vision or the land of the vision.

unwavering faith and obedience (Genesis 22:1-13).[147] Because of this event, the reputation of the rock was further clarified in that it represented sacrifice, substitution, emancipation, and peace building on the reputation established by Melchizedek and his kind. This particular rock was apparently already, at the time of Abraham, widely known as the place for sacrifice. This seems likely since God required Abraham to make an arduous journey to this rock to sacrifice Isaac. Otherwise, it would have been more convenient for Abraham to sacrifice Isaac out behind his tent in Beersheba. Certainly, this would have been more convenient than travelling the three day's journey to Salem to do the deed (Genesis 22:4). Through this incident with Abraham, the rock also came to be associated with belief in God, the most salient characteristic of Abraham (Galatians 3:6),[148] the reason he came to the rock in the first place. Thus, it may not be surprising that belief (confidence) is the requirement stated in Isaiah 28:16 for gaining freedom from the

---

147 Genesis 22: "1 And it came to pass after these things, that God did tempt Abraham, and said unto him, Abraham: and he said, Behold, here I am. 2 And he said, Take now thy son, thine only son Isaac, whom thou lovest, and get thee into the land of Moriah; and offer him there for a burnt offering upon one of the mountains which I will tell thee of. 3 And Abraham rose up early in the morning, and saddled his ass, and took two of his young men with him, and Isaac his son, and clave the wood for the burnt offering, and rose up, and went unto the place of which God had told him. 4 Then on the third day Abraham lifted up his eyes, and saw the place afar off... 10 And Abraham stretched forth his hand, and took the knife to slay his son. 11 And the angel of the LORD called unto him out of heaven, and said, Abraham, Abraham: and he said, Here am I. 12 And he said, Lay not thine hand upon the lad, neither do thou any thing unto him: for now I know that thou fearest God, seeing thou hast not withheld thy son, thine only son from me. 13 And Abraham lifted up his eyes, and looked, and behold behind him a ram caught in a thicket by his horns: and Abraham went and took the ram, and offered him up for a burnt offering in the stead of his son."

148 Gal 3:6 "Even as Abraham believed God," *kathoos Abraam episteusen*, aorist indicative passive of *pisteuo* = down to the fact that the father of many had, no doubt, at one time, confidence, "and it was accounted to him for righteousness." *kai elogisthee*, aorist indicative passive of *logizomai* = and [this confidence] was, no doubt, at one time, logged, inventoried, *auto*, to him, *eis dikasuneen*, into rightness, justness, right relatedness.

Covenant with Death and the resultant self-imposed death tax (the agreement with hell). It may be surprising that this belief/confidence must be in a rock. This rock, however, is a symbol of the stability required for us to handle the fundamental instability in our lives resulting from our mortality."[149]

American Pie,[150] Isaiah 28:16, Romans 9:33b.[151] Each of the two Hebrew words translated as man in the Old Testament implies emotional instability resulting from our mortal state.[152] We are fundamentally insecure and unstable. These twin curses amount to the taxes necessitated by our Covenant with Death. Because confidence is a trait that is rare among humans, we value people who are confident. Confidence is the antidote for instability. It is the underlying condition required for many traits we admire in people including stability, security, tranquility, dependability, and beauty (composure and poise). The trait is so universally admired that many who lack confidence feel it necessary to cover up their associated insecurities. They attempt to accomplish this by substituting arrogance for confidence. Arrogance is a mimic of confidence rooted in insecurity. Even the people we admire the most for their stability and security seem to have a "breaking point". They have their "Achilles heel", some trigger point that "sends them over the edge" causing them to "lose it", letting their emotions get the best

---

149 Isaiah 28:16, "he that believeth shall not make haste" *hama^{a}miyn* = Hiphil [causative] participle of *awman* = English amen, ***he that is holding firm [to the rock] in confidence…****lo-yaachiysh*, Hiphil (causative) imperfect of *chuwsh* = ***will not be*** flushed out, caused to be ***unstable***, agitated, overeager, in a hurry, off in a storm. Stability is a trait particularly treasured among people…

150 "And the three men I admire most - The Father, Son and the Holy Ghost - They took the last train for the coast The day the music died." *American Pie*, 1971, sung and written by Don McLean, in American Pie album, reference to "the day the music died" — the 1959 plane crash that killed Buddy Holly, Ritchie Valens, and Jiles Perry Richardson, Jr.

151 Romans 9:33b "As it is written, Behold, I lay in Sion a stumblingstone and rock of offence: and whosoever believeth on him shall not be ashamed."

152 *Awdawm* as in Adam from *awdawn* = red, to flush with emotion, and *^{a}nash* as in *k^{a}bar ^{a}nash*, the Son of Man, Daniel 7:13 [from *awnash* = frail, feeble, desperate].

of them. As stated earlier in context of the touchstone, the assumption that every man has a point of vulnerability (a point triggering panic) that reveals his underlying insecurity is the basis for the long-term practice of mankind in the use of torture. Although modern man has utilized this procedure (e.g. waterboarding), the Romans in the first century had torture down to a fine art. Although the Romans practiced their fine art on Jesus with great precision, they never found his "panic button". This is the point at which he would be forced to reveal his insecurity. Since Jesus had no insecurity, no amount of torture could reveal insecurity. It can be inferred from the parable of the rich man and Lazarus (Luke 16) that if we do not reach the revelation of our poor deal with mortality in this life, and thereby continue to be unwilling to accept with confidence God's covenant, the resultant insecurities will be revealed during the "torments" in the afterlife. "Torments" is the King James Version of *basanos* which is also translated in extra-biblical Greek as the touchstone, the stone conveniently placed to allow "someone going down" the opportunity to signal that he has reached his threshold of vulnerability and thereby willing to reveal all the insecurities he has worked so hard to hide.[153]

153 Luke 16:23, "And in hell he lift up his eyes, being in torments, and seeth Abraham afar off, and Lazarus in his bosom." The word "hell" translates *hades* from *a* = not, *eido* = having intuitive knowledge. Not only do we not have experiential knowledge (*ginosko*), we don't even have any intuitive knowledge (*eido*) concerning the other side of the grave. However, as we reach that point of no return, this verse indicates that we will come under torment. "Torments", as stated earlier translates *basanos*, the touchstone. It is possible that when we reach that point of no vision of the road ahead (Hades), if we have not done so earlier, we will walk ourselves (be walked?) down to our breaking point and we will gladly touch the stone to find some relief from the bad deal we have made in our Covenant with Death. This kind of torment has a purpose. In this parable the purpose is not to punish, but so that the one being tormented/tortured will confess, show who he is. It is possible that at our death (or after), we will reach the point that we touch the touchstone, indicating we are at the point of revealing that we made a bad deal in our Covenant with Death. If we don't confess this before our death, the parable indicates that, without a guide, left to our own resources, our travels will take us a long way from Abraham down a path toward this revelation, giving meaning to "every knee shall bow and every tongue confess"(Isaiah 45:23; Romans 14:11; Philippians 2:10-11; Hebrews 6:13).

Amen to That, Brother, Isaiah 28:16, Romans 9:33b. I have known Dr. Del Davis, a world recognized livestock nutritionist, since I was nine years old. We showed steers in the same 4-H club and went to the same schools until we received our B.S. degrees at Abilene Christian. He received his PhD at the University of Tennessee before I was on the faculty there. We work together now in China. Fresh out of our PhD programs, we applied for the same research position at the Mississippi Agricultural and Forestry Experiment Station near Greenville, Mississippi. Del is one of the most dependable and secure people I know, solid as a rock. Yet, when he was interviewing for the job in Mississippi, he made air travel reservations for Greenville. The only problem was, on the day scheduled for his interview, when he arrived at his destination, he was in Greenville, North Carolina. I can only conclude that he was "off in a storm" when he made the reservation (must have been a hasty action). Thus, on the day he was to interview in Mississippi he was in North Carolina. He was late for his interview and I got the job. (I flew to Greenville, Mississippi for <u>my</u> interview.) It is one thing to live a stable life with isolated unsettled events as in Del's case, but many people's lives are characterized by chronic instability. Of course it takes only one unstable event to "do you in". In the Old Testament, the value of the opposite trait to man's prevalent condition is reflected by the frequent use of the word amen (Hebrew: *awmane* = let it be stably so, dependable).[154]

Illegal Procedure, Isaiah 28:16, Romans 9:33b. Paul, in both the opening and closing stanzas to his *remez* of Isaiah 28 (Romans 9:33 and 10:11), quoted the Septuagint as "whosoever believeth on him shall not be ashamed" instead of the reading in Isaiah 28:16 of "shall not make

154 *Awmane*, sure, faithful, true [from *awman* = to build up or support, to be quiet, or permanent], used 37 times in Old Testament, KJV. The root of the verb *hama*^{a}*miyn* translates "he that believeth", Isaiah 28:16.

haste".[155] Understanding the connection between making haste and being ashamed requires an analysis of the instability process. Contrary to what we might have thought, Paul says that belief (confidence) in the rock is the only antidote to instability. Although we may try to hide the fact that we are fundamentally instable, certain instances in life occur that require our spontaneous response, causing us to involuntarily reveal that we are not as stable as we might like to appear. Such is the case at times when we are "overeager" (when we make haste). This expression of instability is the picture in American football of the offensive lineman who has no confidence that he is as quick as his defensive opponent. Because he believes his counterpart is quicker than he is, he sometimes "jumps the gun" on the snap count, being overeager. An infraction known in collegiate football as a "false start" is called, resulting in the embarrassment of his number being announced and his team penalized for his hastiness (or more fundamentally his insecurity or nonconfidence).[156] There is a legend about Louis Butman, a pioneering old-time rancher who lived in Mulberry Canyon, a rough shrubland south of Merkel. He was a crusty old codger who lived as a miser and refused to hire hands to help

---

155 Romans 9:33b, "whosoever believeth on him shall not be ashamed" *ho*, ***him that...*** *pistuon* = present active participle of *pisteuo* = ***is*** believing, ***having confidence, being convinced...****ep' auto*, ***upon him [referring to a rock as a him?]...****ou*, ***absolutely not...***, *kataischuntheestetai* = future perfect of *kataischos* = ***will be put to the blush***, [*kata* = down, *aischos* = feel the effect of disfigurement: shame], *The Septuagint with Apocrypha: Greek and English*, 1851, Sir Lancelot C.L.Brenton, Samuel Bagster & Sons, Ltd, London, as compared to the previously quoted Isaiah 28:16, "he that believeth shall not make haste" *hama^a^miyn* = Hiphil [causative] participle of *awman* = English amen, *he that is holding firm [to the rock] in confidence...lo-yaachiysh*, Hiphil (causative) imperfect of *chuwsh* = will not be flushed out, caused to be unstable, agitated, overeager, in a hurry, off in a storm. Stability is a trait particularly treasured among people.

156 So, the translators who wrote the Septuagint as reported in Paul's *remez* translated the Hebrew *yaachiysh* [Hiphil {causative} imperfect of *chuwsh* = to cause to be flushed out and therefore disturbed, agitated and unstable] for "make haste" [KJV] in Isaiah 28:16 in the usual fashion to *kataischuntheestetai* [future perfect of *kataischuno* = be put to the blush] in Greek, and as "be ashamed" [KJV] in English. In Hebrew thinking, being flushed out [making haste] was shameful. We also believe this; thus we have adages such as: "never let them see you sweat".

him on the ranch. The only company he enjoyed was himself. On one of those blustery, west Texas, partly cloudy days, he was oiling one of his Aermotor windmills high above the water trough where his cows gathered to commune. Mr. Butman made the mistake of looking up. The clouds were passing over him at a dizzying rate. He became disoriented, surmised that the windmill must be falling, and escaped impending disaster by jumping off. His family found him a day or two later, a little dehydrated (he was "dried up" anyway), a little red-faced (the sun had burnt his skin anyway), and with a broken leg (he walked with the cowboy swagger anyway). He was a tough old cowboy on the order of Russell's Wagon Boss, and thus he outlasted the incident. But the story outlasted him. Generically, the connection between being hasty and being ashamed is: those who are flushed out of their hiding place before they are ready, caught proverbially with their pants down, are rushed into mistakes that are embarrassing. In the grand scheme of world events, being overeager may seem like a mild infraction. After all, in the NFL, the penalty for the innocuous "illegal procedure" is only five yards. And there can be extenuating circumstances providing excuse for being overeager. A classmate of mine Joe Higgins, who played on the line for the Merkel Badgers in 1965, had a classic excuse for jumping the gun when Merkel played the Roscoe Plowboys. Joe's "assignment" had quite a reputation for being tough. So, when they lined up for the first play from scrimmage, Joe "sneaked a peak" just to get an idea of how tough he looked. His assignment was already looking at Joe, and when he saw Joe looking at him, he grinned. A live lizard was squirming between his teeth. Sometimes, we have good excuses for being overeager. But, as shown in Chapter 1, this state of mind reflects the inner desire for quick self-aggrandizement exalting the desires of the self so that this way of thinking is the basis for all the actions we classify as sin. These actions not only reflect personal instability but also precipitate further destabilization. Being overeager also results in destabilization by setting roadblocks to the fulfillment of the will of God. This overeagerness is an expression that God is taking too long, life is not occurring fast enough;

therefore, the one in the race must take the "bull by the horns" and "make something happen".[157] One can only guess what the world would be like now if Abraham and Sarah, people respected for their faith, had waited on the Lord to create Isaac instead of taking the initiative to create Ishmael.[158] Winston Churchill, during World War II, said "Americans can always be counted on to do the right thing...after they have exhausted all other possibilities." That possibly defines the overeager state of the Covenant with Death. We will trust God… after we have exhausted all other possibilities.

A Poor Deal, Isaiah 28:17-20[159]

"I have squandered my resistance
For a pocketful of mumbles,
Such are promises
All lies and jests"

157 Psalm 25: 2 "O my God, I trust in thee: let me not be ashamed, let not mine enemies triumph over me. 3 Yea, let none that wait on thee be ashamed: let them be ashamed which transgress without cause. 4 Shew me thy ways, O LORD; teach me thy paths. 5 Lead me in thy truth, and teach me: for thou art the God of my salvation; on thee do I wait all the day." Isaiah 40:31 "But they that wait upon the LORD shall renew their strength; they shall mount up with wings as eagles; they shall run, and not be weary; and they shall walk, and not faint."

158 Genesis 16: 2 "And Sarai said unto Abram, Behold now, the LORD hath restrained me from bearing: I pray thee, go in unto my maid; it may be that I may obtain children by her. And Abram hearkened to the voice of Sarai… 11 And the angel of the LORD said unto her, Behold, thou art with child, and shalt bear a son, and shalt call his name Ishmael; because the LORD hath heard thy affliction." "Ishmael" *Yishma'el* = God <u>will</u> hear.

159 Isaiah 28:17 Judgment also will I lay to the line, and righteousness to the plummet: and the hail shall sweep away the refuge of lies, and the waters shall overflow the hiding place. 18 And your Covenant with Death shall be disannulled, and your agreement with hell shall not stand; when the overflowing scourge shall pass through, then ye shall be trodden down by it. 19 From the time that it goeth forth it shall take you: for morning by morning shall it pass over, by day and by night: and it shall be a vexation only to understand the report. 20 For the bed is shorter than that a man can stretch himself on it: and the covering narrower than that he can wrap himself in it.

The Boxer, Paul Simon, 1968, Simon and Garfunkel from *A Midsummer Night's Dream,* 1595, William Shakespeare.

Flirting with Death, Isaiah 28:17. Isaiah paints a vivid picture of the resounding failure of our Covenant with Death in Isaiah 28:17-20. Isaiah 28: 17 states that confidence in the Cornerstone is necessary for us to see with clarity the problem of our deal with mortality.[160] When confidence is expressed in the Cornerstone, we are able to fully comprehend the foolishness of our personal deal with our mortality and the silliness of our hiding the deal from ourselves. The only other possibility for us seeing this truth is at the time we are fully exposed at our deaths (or, as we have seen, when we touch the stone on the other side). From only those perspectives are we in position to perceive how our concept of death (and life) "measure up". The covenant that we worked so hard to develop, paid taxes on for so long, and that we buried so deep in our psyche will be revealed in the "accompanying storm".[161] If we have not developed faith in the Cornerstone by the time of our death, it will, at that time, be revealed to all that we have taken refuge in our own fabrications. We have been telling ourselves repeatedly that our story has merit. So much so, that we began to believe it ourselves. The truth will come out one way or the other. We will see it either at the time we develop confidence in the Cornerstone, or at the time of our death "when the overflowing scourge

---

160 Isaiah 28:17, The connection between confidence and ability to see with clarity is in the phrase, "Judgment also will I lay to the line" *mishpaaT,* ***the verdict, the truth [about our little private covenant, with all its ramifications [taxes]...*** [through the revelation of the Cornerstone, Isaiah 28: 16] *w^a^samtiy,* Wah conjunctive of Qal [active] perfect of *suwm* = ***I will therefore line up to the cord for horizontal measurement of trueness.*** The connection is also in the phrase: "and righteousness to the plummet" *uwtsdaaqaah,* ***justice and rightness [as it contrasts to our covenant]...*** *l^a^mishqaalet,* ***I will line up to the plumb line for vertical measurement of trueness.*** When we have confidence in the cornerstone, everything will fall into place, all will be plumb. Not only will we be able to see it clearly, we will not be able to escape it...

161 Isaiah 28:17, "the hail shall sweep away", *wayaa'aah,* Qal [active] perfect of *yawaw* = ***the hail will easily and completely brush aside...*** "the refuge of lies", *kawzab,* ***the shelter of our [former] deceitfulness...***

shall pass through". Instead of "it shall not come unto us" (Isaiah 28:15) as our self-deception would have it, the reality is that "the waters shall overflow the hiding place" (Isaiah 28:17).[162] When these things come to light for all to see, the foolishness of our deal with our mortality, including all the taxes we have paid during our lives, will be presented to all. This revelation will provide the basis for our redness of face. We will be flushed out and forced to find another hiding place.

O Lord, Won't You Buy Me a Mercedes Benz?,[163] Isaiah 28:17. When I was born in Abilene, Texas, my parents had already survived the dust bowl, the great depression and two world wars so, comparatively, we were doing well on our dry-land farm near Merkel raising cotton, sorghum, chickens and cattle during the long drought and periodic dust storms of the 1950s. It was important not to spend money on frivolous items and to make best use of the resources we had. This frugality was evidenced in our clothing. As was the custom of that era among "share-croppers"[164], some of my shirts were made from chicken feed sacks. I learned just how much we were willing to spend on my wardrobe when my mother took me shopping in Abilene for my first pair of cowboy boots. At the time, at least in my mind, it was not hard to know what good cowboy boots were. They were the ones with a lot of decorative stitching. Of course these boots were also the most expensive. Although I had my heart set on a pair with comparable stitching to boots my friends at school wore, my mother was not impressed with either the stitching or the price. So, after a heated debate (I can't remember ever winning an argument with my mother), we bought the under-stitched boots. Well, they became

162 Isaiah 28:17, "the waters shall overflow the hiding place", *yshTaduw*, Qal [active] imperfect of *shawtaf* = ***the flood will inundate, making transparent,*** cleansing... *w^aceeter* = ***your covert cover...***

163 *Mercedes Benz*, 1971, written by Janis Joplin, Michael McClure, and Bob Neuwirth, sung by Janis Joplin, album *Pearl*, Written October 1, 1970 three days before Janis Joplin's death from a drug overdose.

164 "Share-croppers: Farmers who rent land for a share of the crop." *The American Heritage Dictionary of the English Language*, 1969, William Morris, Editor, American Heritage Publishing Co., Boston, MA, ISBN 395-09064-4.

an Albatross[165] around my neck. Every time I wore them, I imagined that my friends were looking sideways at them. I thought I caught one or two snickering at them. I was ashamed of the boots and that shame overflowed into a shame for myself and who I was. I admit I carried it too far. But, I thought the boot purchase was a bad deal, and I was ashamed of the deal, the boots, and ultimately myself. Thus, it will be when we have to face the music concerning the biggest bad deal we can make in this life, our personal "arrangement" with our mortality. In the case of Isaiah 28:16, those holding firmly to the rock, having confidence in Him concerning their journey, will always be confident. They will never be "caught out", not even in the most personal experience possible, death. They will never have a reason to be embarrassed. On the other hand, those who take matters into their own hands and make their own deal with their mortality and thus pay their own private death tax will one day be found out. Their personal deal will be shown to be what it is: flawed. And nothing is more embarrassing than making a bad deal, whether the deal is for boots, a car, or for a life. So, how is it that we will be found out?

A New Covenant, Isaiah 28:18. The picture in this recap of previous verses illustrates the pride we had in our contract with death that we fostered by self-deception, hiding, even from ourselves, any reservation that we had about it. The contract itself was the lie that we can escape death. We admit that death will come, but we lie to ourselves by thinking that we can somehow hide from it. This lie is compounded by the fact that we are in deep denial that we are living this lie. Because of this compounded lie, we have to pay the death tax amounting to guilt, fear and doubt. These deceptions, however, come naturally to us. After all, we had much invested in the contract. It had become integrally entwined with our ego. Our contract also seemed intuitively correct in terms of

165 "Are those her ribs through which the Sun, Did peer, as through a grate? And is that Woman all her crew? Is that a DEATH? and are there two? Is DEATH that woman's mate?" *The Rime of the Ancient Mariner,* 1798, Samuel Taylor Coleridge.

our perspective of the world. As Harvard neuro-opthomologist, Dr. Dean Cestari said, "anticipating the expected can 'blind' onlookers to the unexpected".[166] We are often deceived by appearances, expectations, and assumptions. Our expectations can affect not only what we feel is the truth, but also what is actually truth. In medicine, the placebo effect has been shown not only to alter how a person feels, but also to alter how a person is.[167] If we know death is final, we may actually alter our physiology, neurology and endocrinology accordingly. But our contract with death was shown to be critically and terminally flawed. We had paid the escalating tax (more like ransom) for years and, when the poor bargain was revealed, our faces were red with shame (Romans 9:33,10:11). At the time of revelation, our agreement with our mortality will not withstand the scrutiny allowed by the glaring light of the revealed truth.[168] But, fortunately for us, God understood our flawed deal and provided a way out for us through the laying of a stone. Belief in this stone somehow wrote over (erased and replaced) the poor contract we had made with our mortality. Therefore, if we have confidence in the Cornerstone, our death deal becomes null and void. In that case, at the time of our death, the only thing of importance is that our silly little death deal is no longer remembered because the Cornerstone "whited out" (cut and pasted?) our deal with a new writing.[169] The fact that we ever made this silly little deal in the first place is so overshadowed by our new deal that no one

166 Quoted in *USA Today*, "Ever ask how'd he do that?" by Mary Marcus, October 20, 2009.

167 "Placebo effect can help believers" by Marilynn Marchione, Associated Press in the *San Antonio Express-News*, November 11, 2009.

168 Isaiah 28:18, "your agreement with hell shall not stand" *w^{a}chaazuwt^{a}kem*, Wah conjunctive of *khawzuth* = ***your compact…***'*et-Shaowl* = ***with the place of the dead…****lo' taaquwm*, Qal imperfect of *quwm* = ***will not continue to stand up [under scrutiny]…***

169 Isaiah 28:18, "your Covenant with Death shall be disannulled" *w^{a}kupar*, Wah conjunctive, Pual [passive] perfect of *kawfar* = ***Thereby your death deal will be*** covered over, ***cancelled***, propitiated, pacified, atoned for (A word used for cancellation of a contract by writing over the old wording, not only blotting out the old writing, but replacing the old with new writing, in this case, a New Covenant.)…

even remembers we were ever so foolish as to deceive ourselves in that manner.

The Proof of the Pudding, Isaiah 28:18-20. Isaiah, however, is relentless in his demonstration of the embarrassing disclosure of our private deal with death. If we do not develop the required confidence in the Cornerstone, the *coup de grace* will occur at our death when our Covenant with Death will be fully exposed to be a bad deal because of the very fact of our death.[170] At that time, when our bad deal is put under the spotlight in comparison to the good deal offered by God, which we either refused or ignored, we will not be able to escape the stark truth that our concocted, *ad hoc* deal was actually ridiculous. The truth will dog our every move.[171] At that time, we will be thunderstruck and full of remorse for not taking the deal offered to us by God.[172] We will realize that our approach to the problem was woefully inadequate. This inadequacy, like an uncomfortable bed, cannot be ignored though we might try to ignore it. The inadequacy is similar to having to sleep in a bed that is too short with a blanket that is too narrow (or perhaps trying

170 Isaiah 28: 19, "when the overflowing scourge shall pass through," *ShowT showTeep, **the lashing lash...**ya^a^bor,* Qal [active] imperfect of *awbar'* = ***will begin to cross over the bar...*** "then ye shall be trodden down by it." *wih^a^yiytem,* Wah conjunctive Qal [active] perfect of *hayah* = ***it will come to pass that...**l^a^mirmaac,* ***it will walk all over you...***

171 Isaiah 28:19, "From the time that it goeth forth" *middee,* ***It is substantially sufficient, abundant...**aab^a^row,* Qal [active] infinitive construct of *'abar* = ***to pass over, to cross over...*** "it shall take you" *yiqach,* Qal [active] imperfect of *lawkach* = ***it will begin to*** impregnate, take hold, destabilize, ***unsettle you...*** *'etkem,* ***intimately and personally...*** "for morning by morning it will pass over" *kiy baboqer baboqer,* ***it is as sure as the day will break...*** [from the breaking to the breaking] *ya^a^bor,* Qal [active] imperfect of *abar'* ***it will continue to inundate you...*** "by day and by night" *bayowm' uwbalaay^a^laah,* ***[as certain as] the heat of the day and the calamity of night...***

172 Isaiah 28:19, "and it shall be a vexation only to understand the report" *w^a^haayaah,* Qal [active] perfect of *hawyaw'* = ***it will come to exist...**raq-,* ***at the least...*** *z^a^waa'aah,* ***as an agitation, something difficult to shake off...*** *Haabiyn,* Hiphil [causative] infinitive construct of *biyn* = ***just to be able to give understanding to...**sh^a^muw'aah,* feminine passive participle of *shawmame* = the announcement, ***the revelation*** that stuns or numbs, causing one to feel thunderstruck...

to sleep in an economy seat on a transpacific flight). If we stretch out to relax, our feet hang off the bed. If we pull our feet up to compensate for the short bed, then the narrow blanket exposes either our rear end or our knees to the cold. We just can't, at that point, get comfortable. We had made a bad deal when we purchased the bed and blanket, and now we are forced to admit that poor deal. We had glossed over these problems earlier, not coming to grips with them until it was time to go to bed (too late to remedy the problem). We end up with sleepless nights, tossing and turning, trying to "make do" with a deal that we are not willing to admit was bad from the beginning.[173] Our death bed will not be (emotionally) comfortable on that day unless we prepare for it by making the right deal before then. Sooner or later we will be forced to admit we made a bad deal during life.

173 Isaiah 28:20, "for the bed is shorter than a man can stretch himself on it" *kiy-* ***forasmuch as...****qarsar* ***the curtailed...****hamatsaa*, couch, ***place of rest...****mee histaareea*, Hithpael [result presented in reflexive voice] infinitive construct of *sawrah'* = ***[we found it difficult] to extend contracted and fatigued muscles*** "and the covering narrower than that can wrap himself in it" *w*^{a}*hamaceekaah*, Wah consecutive: ***not only that but the coverlet...****tsaaraah*, ***cramps***, restricts, binds, is scant...*k*^{a}*hitkaneec*, Hithpael [result presented in reflexive voice] infinitive construct of *kawnas* = ***[when we try] to enfold, wrap it around us...***

CHAPTER 4

THE COVENANT WITH LIFE: TAKING THE EDGE OFF

Fleshing Out the Rock, Romans 10:1-4[174]

"Rock of Ages, cleft for me,
Let me hide myself in thee;
Let the water and the blood,
From thy wounded side which flowed,
Be of sin the double cure;
Save from wrath and make me pure."

> *Rock of Ages, Gospel Magazine,* 1775, Augustus Montague Toplady.

Rocked by the Rock, Romans 10:1-2. It might be easy to disassociate Romans 10 from Romans 9, as did the scribe who added the chapter breaks to the manuscript, if we could ignore several signals in the text linking the two. One signal linking the two chapters is Paul's referral to Isaiah 28:16 both in Romans 9:33 and in 10:11 giving evidence to

174 Romans 10: "1 Brethren, my heart's desire and prayer to God for Israel is, that they might be saved. 2 For I bear them record that they have a zeal of God, but not according to knowledge. 3 For they being ignorant of God's righteousness, and going about to establish their own righteousness, have not submitted themselves unto the righteousness of God. 4 For Christ is the end of the law for righteousness to every one that believeth."

the unity of the intervening discussion. The second signal is the series of Greek words in Romans 10:1 that are each difficult to translate into English and therefore are omitted in all translations.[175] Those small, untranslated words undeniably tie the discussion of Romans 10:1-11 to Romans 9:33 and thus to the Covenant with Death. This scripture is similar to all the rest of Paul's writings in the New Testament; each verse is connected to the other verses in a cascade of thought concurrently expanding in multiple dimensions and running from 9:33 to 10:11 (and beyond).[176] It is apparent that Paul is adding depth to the Jewish concept of the stone God laid in Zion. At the first of Chapter 10, Paul expressed his concern for Israel although the Greek text only obliquely indicates he is talking about them.[177] His prayer for them was "that they might be saved".[178] The question is, what do they need to be saved from? The answer in context with Paul's *remez* can only be that they need to be saved from their Covenant with Death. In this respect, and as Paul says in Romans 10:12, we are all alike, Jew and Gentile. We are also all alike in respect that we have a "zeal for God".[179] Israel possibly possessed an extreme form of curiosity and intrigue about God of a type that

---

175 Romans 10:1 "Brethren, my hearts desire...is" *Adelphoi*, ***those in my circumstance...****mee hoi* [the untranslated words in both the Textus Receptus and The Nestle Text] ***because of this thing...*** referring to Romans 9:33 and thus Isaiah 28, our Covenant with Death and God's response...*eudokia*, ***the delight...****emees*, ***of my ...****kardias*, ***core...***

176 As the KJV indicates through the connecting words from 10:2 to 10:12: For, For, For, For, But, Or, But, That, For, For, For.

177 Romans 10:1 "Brethren, my heart's desire and prayer to God for Israel" Although the word "Israel" is omitted in the Greek text, referred to only as *autoon* = them, the term "brethren" is reserved by Paul to his Israeli brothers, *adelphoi* = out of the same womb, or being in similar circumstance...

178 Romans 10:1 "that they might be saved" *eis sooteerion*, into safety, ***is deliverance...***

179 Romans 10:2 "For I bear them record" *Marturoo*, present indicative of *martureo* = ***I*** now testify, ***continue to give witness...****gar*, ***the reason [I am for their deliverance] is...***"that they have a zeal for God" *hoti*, ***that...****zeelon*, gusto, ***fervor...****Theou*, ***for God...****echousin*, present indicative of *echo* = ***they hold onto...***

is common to all of us. We are all possessed with a wonder about the possibility of an unseen force at work in the world. "Spirituality" is a popular cult in the modern era as is evidenced by the many movies and books available concerning the supernatural and especially the possibility that we might become supernatural. We are obsessed with the "unseen". Many examples in film include the *Harry Potter* series, *The Lord of the Rings* series, *The X-Files* series, the *Transformers* series, the *Pirates of the Caribbean* series, and the multiple *Batman* series, *etc.* We are extremely curious about the possibility of the spirit world. Some of us are zealous about exploring this possibility. In this passage, Paul indicated that, in order to overcome our Covenant with Death, we must carry our zeal beyond a passive interest in exploring the spiritual. We must become actively involved with God. Thus, in order to take advantage of the reprieve provided by God from our Covenant with Death, we must have experience with the Rock. We must allow the Rock to rock our world. But, as Paul says of the first century Jews, we fall short in terms of interactive experience ("knowledge") in this arena.[180]

Agnosticism: Ignorance is Bliss, Romans 10:3-4. Although the Jews in first century Rome lacked experiential knowledge of God (*gnosis*), they did have intuitive knowledge of God (*eido*), but it did them little good in escaping their Covenant with Death.[181] We are similar to the Roman Jews that Paul was addressing. We intuitively feel the spiritual realm, but it is just beyond our reach. Science cannot explore the nature of the spirit realm or of God. Therefore, we are like the Jews, having no data about God, we go our own way, trying to do the best we can with

180 Romans 10:2, "but not according to knowledge" *all'*, ***to the contrary,...****ou*, ***[this fervor is] absolutely not...****kat*, ***down to...****epigoosin*, ***the basis of personal experiential recognition...*** [*epi* = upon, *ginosko* = experiential knowledge, the other Greek word translated as knowledge is *eido* = intuitive knowledge]...

181 Romans 10:3 "For they being ignorant of God's righteousness" *agnontes*, present active participle of *agnosis* = ***Having no experiential knowledge...*** [a = no, ginosko = experiential knowledge, Latin nosko, novi, English novice] being agnostic...*gar*, ***[as the basis for their fervor]...****teen tou Theou dikaiosuneen*, ***in the rightness of God...***

what little hard data we can muster. Left to ourselves, we have to make the best deal we can with our mortality and, in that way, we attempt to establish our own rightness.[182] When confronted with the barrier of death and the need to formulate a method to live sanely in the face of this barrier, we have only two possible avenues for formulating a plan: we can have confidence in ourselves to get us out of this mess, or we can have confidence in God to extricate us. If we have confidence in ourselves, in our ability to make the right decisions about our mortal lives, we are, in essence, saying that we can live "right" through our own resources. In following this path, we demonstrate the trait many mortals seek, the trait of self-confidence. If we rely on our own deal with mortality, we won't rely on God for a solution.

We Did It Our Way, Romans 10:3-4. It only seems natural for us to seek our own way to being right with respect to our mortality. In tune with that way, we decide the appropriate way to live.[183] Frank Sinatra is not the only one who "did it my way". We are likely to be the most demanding of our right to do it our way (being rebellious) at the times in our lives when either internal or external changes remind us, at least subconsciously, of our mortality. As Nancy Gibbs in an essay for *Time* magazine asks, "What is a midlife crisis if not an adolescent rebellion with a bigger price tag?"[184] The sticking point for us in turning over our confidence to

---

182 Romans 10:3, "and going about to establish their own righteousness" *kai teen*, ***[they pursue the only other] alternative*** [there is only one other alternative to experiencing God's right way of the Cornerstone] as...*idian*, ***their own private, exclusive, personal, clubish, secret path to...*** [*idian* is the word used to describe their method instead of the alternatives of either *demosios* = open, democratic or *koinos* = in common]... *dikaiosuneen*, justness, ***the status of being right [in their dealings with mortality]...*** *zeetountes*, present active participle of zeteo = endeavoring, plotting, ***in striving to find...*** *steesai*, aorist infinitive of *histimai* = ***a place to stand*** [English: stasis, static]...

183 Romans 10:3 "have not submitted themselves unto the righteousness of God" *tee dikaiosunee*, emphatically, ***the rightness of God...*** *ouch*, ***absolutely in no way...*** *hupatageesan*, aorist indicative passive of *hupotasso* = ***did they subordinate themselves.*** [*hupo* = to place under, *tasso* = in order, to line up]...

184 Nancy Gibbs, *Time* Essay, *Time*, February 8, 2009.

God is that we must give up the control we establish by making our own personal deal with our mortality. We not only have to give up control, but we also must accept the seemingly vague concept that belief in the Cornerstone is the right way for us to deal with mortality. As inadequate as our way may appear when scrutinized in broad daylight,[185] it seems to us to be better than the vagueness of trusting in the Cornerstone. Paul gave clarity and understanding to the meaning of the Cornerstone by revealing that the Cornerstone is Christ.[186] The Cornerstone is not only the foundation of the law and a waymarker/milestone on life's journey, He is the goal of the law. The law did not make man right with God, did not solve man's problem with mortality; but it did point to the justness of the Cornerstone who was anointed by God for the purpose of freeing man from his bad deal, thereby giving him the right perspective on life. All we have to do is have confidence in Him.[187]

Higher and Higher, Romans 10:5-7[188]

"Blasting, billowing, bursting forth,
With the power of ten billion butterfly sneezes,
Man, with his flaming pyre,
Has conquered the wayward breezes,"

---

185 As shown in Isaiah 28:17-20 as explained in the previous chapter.

186 Romans 10:4 "For Christ is the end of the law" *Telos*, emphatically, ***the goal,*** aim, limit, destination, conclusion, result [English example, telephone = *telos*, the goal of...*phone'*, the voice]...*gar,* ***[by way of] the reason*** [they did not subordinate themselves to God]...*nomou,* ***of the law***...*Christos,* ***is the anointed one, the Messiah...***

187 Romans 10:4 "for righteousness to everyone who believeth" *eis,* ***into...*** *dikaiosuneen,* rightness, ***equity...****panti,* ***to each and every one, Jew or gentile...*** *too pisteuonti,* present active participle of pisteuo = ***that are trusting, having confidence [in the goal of the law],*** taken by many as a stumblingstone inhibiting life, not facilitating it...

188 Romans 10: "5 For Moses describeth the righteousness which is of the law, That the man which doeth those things shall live by them. 6 But the righteousness which is of faith speaketh on this wise, Say not in thine heart, Who shall ascend into heaven? (that is, to bring Christ down from above:) 7 Or, Who shall descend into the deep? (that is, to bring up Christ again from the dead)."

Higher and Higher in the album *To our Children's Children*, Graeme Edge, 1969, The Moody Blues.

The Riddler,[189] Romans 10:5-7. But, does it make sense that our deliverance from our covenant with mortality can be accomplished by confidence in something so difficult to grasp as the Cornerstone/Christ? Paul shows us that he is addressing this question by beginning Romans 10:5 with the word "For" giving the reason that Christ, the Cornerstone is the goal of the law, the solution to our mortality problem.[190] Paul resorts to the ultimate authority on these matters, the law giver, Moses and to the law itself.[191] Paul spotlights an astounding revelation made by Moses in Leviticus 18:5. Here, Moses states that any man who perpetually performs the law will perpetually live.[192] Leviticus 18:5 indicates that the purpose of the law is to sustain or resurrect life. So, throw away your jogging shoes, sell your stationary bicycle, stop your purchase order for lycopene; all you have to do to cheat death is to keep the law.

189 *Batman Forever,* 1995, film directed by Joel Schumacher, produced by Tim Burton, starring Val Kilmer as Batman and Jim Carrey as the Riddler.

190 Romans 10:5 "For" *gar,* ***the reason [that Christ culminates the law for those having confidence] being...***

191 Romans 10:5 "Moses describeth the righteousness which is of the law" *Moousees,* ***He*** who is drawn out [of the water] or ***who draws*** [people] ***out...****graphei,* present indicative of grapho = ***continues to engrave*** [at least the effect of his engraving continues]...*teen dikaiosuneen,* the defined equity, ***the true meaning of what it is to be right...****ek tou nomou,* ***out of the law,*** the allotment...

192 Romans 10:5, "that the man which doeth those things" *hoti,* ***that...****ho,* ***this one...****poieesis,* aorist participle active of *poieo* = ***having executed,*** performed [Latin *efficio*] having fashioned...*auta,* ***these things [the law]...****anthropos,* ***as a human***: Paul was referring to Moses' law in Leviticus 18:5: "Ye shall therefore keep my statutes" *uwshmartem,* Qal perfect of *shawmar* = you will actively, completely take charge of, pay close attention to...*etchuqutay,* my personal appointment for you "and my judgments" *mishpaaTay,* and pronouncements to you. Then Paul continues in Romans 10:5: "shall live by them" *zeesetai,* future middle of *zao* = ***[this man] will perpetually take his zest,*** his vitality, his life... *en autois,* ***in them...***again referring to Leviticus 18:5 "he shall live in them. I am the Lord." *wa^a^chay,* Wah conjunctive, Qal perfect of *chawyah'ee,* his life will be actively self-perpetuated, sustained, revived, made eternal...*baahem,* by means of them [the law]...

Unfortunately, Paul has already thought through this and has concluded in Romans 3:23 that "all have sinned and come short of the glory of God". No one (other than Christ) can keep the law, adequately living up to God's standard, His law. So, does this mean we have no chance for perpetual life? Or, is there some glimmer of hope in this writing by the law giver? How does the purpose of the law (perpetual life) relate to the goal of the law (the Cornerstone)? If someone was to show us what it is to perpetually keep the law, wouldn't (according to the authority everyone accepts, Moses) that someone also demonstrate that perpetual life is more than an abstract thought and is actually possible? In addition, if that person was resurrected to live perpetually, wouldn't His experiences be valuable to us in our plight to deal with both sides of the grave? Furthermore, wouldn't the precedent set by the demonstrator of these things have direct bearing on the future of our own (possibly perpetual) existence? Questions, questions, there are too many questions.

A Bridge Too Far,[193] **Romans 10:5.** These questions need to be answered if we expect to travel across the barrier of death confidently. At least we need a guide who can answer these questions in order for us to confidently traverse that barrier. Paul, in Romans 10:1-11 addresses these questions and points to that guide. Today, as born out in movies such as *Hereafter*, we pay close attention to descriptions given by people who have had near death experiences. We would like to believe that these experiences can give us glimpses of the other side of death. I was in Ruiz Cafe in the south Texas town of Encinal when I met a cowboy who said that he had died twice. I will admit that, as best I could see him in the dim light of the café, he looked the part: having a certain haggard, haunted appearance like that of a refugee or a desperado, like he had been out riding fences way too long.[194] He said that

193 *A Bridge Too Far*, 1974, Cornelius Ryan inspired by Operation Market Garden in World War II.

194 "Desperado, why don't you come to your senses? You been out ridin' fences for so long now,…These things that are pleasin' you, Can hurt you somehow." *Desperado*, 1973, sung by the Eagles, written by Glenn Frey and Don Henley, album *Desperado*.

the first time he died, he was in M.D. Anderson Hospital in Houston, Texas, and was declared dead on the operating table during open heart surgery. He remembered hovering above the operating table, seeing the back of the surgeon's head, being drawn higher and higher toward a bright light, then walking in a grassy meadow toward a river, being drawn to a white house on the other side. He said that the second time he died, he didn't go much of anywhere. I told him that he was the only person I had ever known who died and went to Kentucky and, what's more, was able to tell of his experience. I also told him that, judging from his appearance, it must be hard on a person to die. He said dying was not a problem; coming back was the hard part. Surely he is right, but Leviticus 18:5 indicates that coming back (and living on) is reserved for that special Person who has perpetually kept the law (with no lapse). As Paul implied in Romans 10:6-7, Christ lived that life, but if He has perpetual life, where is He? Who has the ability to find Him? We know He was around for a while, but if He has experience on both sides of the (head)stone, then we have a few questions we would like to ask Him to rest our fevered brow about the whole subject of mortality.

Curiouser and Curiouser,[195] **Romans 10:6-7a.** So, many people have a curiosity about Christ; He remains in the eyes of many as one of the most enigmatic people to have ever lived. Many want to "peel back the layers to find the historical Jesus".[196] Paul points out that this curiosity (i.e. our need to retrieve the body of Christ) is not consistent with confidence that God will pull us through.[197] Isaiah 28 made it abundantly clear that our resources to formulate a sound plan to deal with our mortality are woefully deficient; our only hope is that God will see us through (to

---

195 *Alice's Adventures in Wonderland*, 1865, Charles Lutwidge Dodgson (Lewis Carroll).

196 e.g. "The Secrets of Christianity, the Real Jesus, A Need to Know Him", 2011, Amy D. Bernstein, *U.S. News and World Report;* and *Excavating Jesus, Beneath the Stones, Behind the Texts,* 2001, John Dominic Crossan and Jonathan L. Reed, HarperCollins Publishers Inc., New York, NY, ISBN 0-06-061633-4.

197 Romans 10:6, "But the righteousness which is of faith" *de,* ***the bottom line that originates...****hee...ek pisteoos,* ***out of our confidence...*** *dikaiosunee,* ***about right relatedness,*** being in the groove, on track with God...

the other side of the grave). Paul illustrates our problem in personally solving the issue of our mortality problem (transcending the barrier of death) by pointing to our inability to cross the less daunting barriers of the sky or the deep sea. First, he points out the obvious limitation that we have in crossing the impenetrable barrier of the sky.[198] Until we learn how to travel faster than the speed of light, we will be unable to cross this barrier to even explore our nearest neighbor solar system. Paul then (with considerable sarcasm) says that man even has difficulty with transportation on this planet, a step back from the problem of transcending the heavens.[199] If we can't cross these relatively simple barriers, how can we even contemplate going through the semipermeable membrane of death…and live to tell about it. In order to understand

---

198 Romans 10:6 "speaketh on this wise" *houtos*, ***in this way…****legei*, present indicative active of lego = ***continues, no doubt, to lay forth:…***, appropriating again the words of Moses in the Septuagint translation of Deuteronomy 30:4-14 "Say not in thine heart" *meh*, ***It is preferable that you do not…****eipes*, aorist subjunctive used as an imperative [forbids an action not in progress] of *epo* = ***speak it…****en tee kardia sou*, ***in the core of you, your essential nature…*** "Who shall ascend into heaven?" *Tis*, ***Which man…****anabeesetai*, future middle of *anabaino* = ***shall for his own sake walk up…*** [*ana* = up, *baino* = to pace] *eis ton ourano*, ***into the sky, eternity?***

199 Romans 10:7a. "Or, Who shall ascend into the deep?" *ee*, ***or rather…****Tis*, ***Who is it?****…katabeesetai*, future middle of *katabaino* = ***will, for his own sake, walk down…*** [*kata* = down, *baino* = to pace]…*eis teen 'abusson*, ***into the abyss*** [*a* = not, *bathos* = a bottom, sea was a mystery, seemingly with no bottom] referring to Deuteronomy 30:13 "Neither is it beyond the sea," *mee[e]ber*, on the other side, trans to the…*yawm*, roar [of the crashing waves]. Paul upped the ante to the challenge provided by Moses in "that thou shouldest say, Who shall go over the sea for us," *ya[a]baar*, Qal [active] imperfect of *awbar'* = who will begin the awesome task of crossing over…*laanow*, parenthetically, who would care that much about us as to begin such an arduous and dangerous task? *eleeber, hayaam*, over on the far shore across the billows…". The deep is beyond our reach. The more we know about it, the more unfathomable it seems. The lowest point in the world on dry land is the Dead Sea (surface at 1,388 ft. below sea level). The lowest point of the ocean is the Challenger Deep in the Mariana Trench, east of the Mariana Islands in the Pacific (6.85 mi. below sea level). http://en.wikipedia.org/wiki/Dead_Sea.

Paul's illustration clearly, we must study the passage to which he alluded, Deuteronomy 30:4-13.[200]

Crossing the Bar, Romans 10:6-7, Deuteronomy 30:4-13[201]

"For though from out our bourn of Time and Place
The flood may bear me far,
I hope to see my Pilot face to face
When I have crost the bar."
Crossing the Bar, 1889, Alfred, Lord Tennyson.

Restaurant at the End of the Universe,[202] Romans 10:6, Deuteronomy 30:4. Eternity is just too great an expanse for our feeble abilities to fathom, much less to traverse. Einstein in his treatise "Relativity: The Special and

---

200 Although Paul alludes to Deuteronomy 30:4-14, some of this passage in Deuteronomy refers to immediate promises God made to the children of Israel as they entered the Promised Land. Paul was making reference to the more transcendent principles in this passage, so I will limit this discussion to those transcendent portions of this passage: Deuteronomy 30:4, 6, 10-13.

201 Romans 10: "6 But the righteousness which is of faith speaketh on this wise, Say not in thine heart, Who shall ascend into heaven? (that is, to bring Christ down from above:) 7 Or, Who shall descend into the deep? (that is, to bring up Christ again from the dead.)"
Deuteronomy 30: "4 If any of thine be driven out unto the outmost parts of heaven, from thence will the LORD thy God gather thee, and from thence will he fetch thee:...6 And the LORD thy God will circumcise thine heart, and the heart of thy seed, to love the LORD thy God with all thine heart, and with all thy soul, that thou mayest live....10 If thou shalt hearken unto the voice of the LORD thy God, to keep his commandments and his statutes which are written in this book of the law, and if thou turn unto the LORD thy God with all thine heart, and with all thy soul. 11 For this commandment which I command thee this day, it is not hidden from thee, neither is it far off. 12 It is not in heaven, that thou shouldest say, Who shall go up for us to heaven, and bring it unto us, that we may hear it, and do it? 13 Neither is it beyond the sea, that thou shouldest say, Who shall go over the sea for us, and bring it unto us, that we may hear it, and do it?"

202 *The Restaurant at the End of the Universe*, 1980, Douglas Adams, 2nd of pentalogy entitled *Hitchhiker's Guide to the Galaxy*. Pan Books, London, ISBN 0-345-39181-0.

General Theory" alluded to the probability that in the universe, some peculiar physical anomalies exists such as wormholes, strings, and black holes.[203] These anomalies are very difficult to imagine, much less to experience personally. But, as Paul quoting Moses points out, in contrast to man, nothing is too hard for the Lord.[204] God can transcend any barrier to retrieve His own.[205] After all, He created these barriers. He can even transcend the barriers of the heart, providing personal focus and motivation powerful enough to impact many people, even those not having been born yet.[206] We are left standing in awe of many of these barriers created by God. Of most pertinence, we stand in awe of the wall we call death. This wall is so formidable that we can't see beyond it. So, even though we feel that the great adversary death is too much for our feeble resources, we do have friends in high places. Death is "no step for a stepper", no problem to God who can transcend not only any barrier that we have experienced but also any barrier that we can imagine.

Let's Go to Luckenbach, Texas,[207] Romans 10:6-7, Deuteronomy 30:6, 10-13. The key as to why we cannot transcend the barrier of death is that

---

203 *Relativity: The Special and General Theory,* 1920, Albert Einstein, New York, NY: Henry Holt; Bartleby.com, 2000. www.bartleby.com/173.

204 Genesis 18:14 "Is any thing too hard for the LORD? At the time appointed I will return unto thee, according to the time of life, and Sarah shall have a son" and in Deuteronomy 30:4-14.

205 Deuteronomy 30:4 "If any one of thine be driven out" *yih[a]yeh,* Qal imperfect of *hawyah'* = ***If any of yours begins to exist as...****nid[a]ch[a]kaa,* Niphal participle of *nawdach'* = **expelled, being banished...** "unto the uttermost parts" *biqtseeh,* ***unto the*** extremities, edges, peripheries, ***remoteness...*** "from thence will the Lord thy God gather thee" *yaq[a]bits[a]kaa* = Piel imperfect of *kawbats'* = ***the Lord will increasingly collect and assemble this one [you]...*** "and from thence fetch thee" *yiqaachikaa,* Qal [active] imperfect of *lawkakh'* = ***and will increasingly snatch this one [you] from there...***

206 Deuteronomy 30:6a "and the Lord thy God will circumcise thine heart" *uwmaal,* Qal [active] perfect of *mool* = ***[The Lord] will*** curtail, ***prune to increase effectiveness***/productivity ***of...****labaabkaa,* ***your essential core...*** "and the heart of thy seed" *zerakaa,* ***and your posterity,*** your sowing...

207 *Luckenbach Texas (Back to the Basics of Love),* 1977, written by Chips Morman and Bobby Emmons, sung by Waylon Jennings and Willie Nelson, album *The Ultimate Waylon Jennings.*

we fail to understand the message emanating from the fact of death. We fail to grasp this message because it is imbedded in a tremendous amount of noise. We find it impossible to distinguish the signal of death's message from this noise. This is true because we are the ones who create the noise through our Covenant with Death. We must cut through the noise and return to what is important ("Back to the Basics of Love"). As an overgrown grape vine needs to be pruned to improve fruitfulness, so God will prune us so we can focus on only the important issues and understand the message of death.[208] Only a few things are important in focusing our lives and in delivering us from our covenant with mortality. These are summed up by Moses in three words that embody the message of death: love, call, and live. First, it is imperative that we believe that God loves us, that no matter what we do or what happens to us that He will come to rescue us, and therefore, we must love Him. If death can be viewed as a barrier, all can agree that the barrier is both formidable and personal. God's purpose in transcending barriers He has created is that He might retrieve us, even from the other side of the His most formidable barrier, the grave. The fact that God has done what was required to retrieve us from death means that He truly loves us and that He deserves our love.[209] Second, out of His love for us, He will give us an important mission that transcends death (our call), and through responding to His call, we will be delivered from our deal with our

208 To reiterate: Romans 10:3 "have not submitted themselves unto the righteousness of God" *tee dikaiosunee*, emphatically, the rightness of God…*ouch*, absolutely in no way… *hupatageesan*, aorist indicative passive of hupotasso = did they subordinate themselves. [*hupo* = to place under, *tasso* = in order, to line up.

209 Deuteronomy 30:6b, "to love the Lord thy God" *l^{a}ah^{a}baah*, Qal [active] infinitive construct of *awhab'* = ***to have affection [as the purpose of the paring] toward…*** *et-Yahweh Eloheykaa*, ***the Almighty in person…*** "with all thy heart and with all thy soul" *b^{a}kaal l^{a}baabkaa uwbkaal nephsh^{a}kaa*, ***to give it your totality and vitality…***

mortality and from mortality itself.[210] Third, if we love Him and respond to His call, we can live perpetual, abundant lives; we need the life on the other side of the grave to pursue our call holistically.[211] Thus, the signal of death is that God's love transcends death (He loves us on both sides of the grave), His call transcends death (our mission/journey encompasses both sides of the grave) and the life He gives transcends death (we can live perpetually). In referring to Deuteronomy 30:11, Paul points out that the chasms that God finds easy to transcend, we find to be impossible to bridge. As Einstein said, reality is a matter of perspective. If we take on the perspective of God, we have no trouble understanding that bridging the expanse of the heavens/eternity is not a problem.[212] This brings up possibly the biggest potential barrier of all, the gap between our perspective and that of the Creator of the universe.[213] God has bridged even this gap;

---

210 Deuteronomy 30:10 "If thou shalt hearken unto the voice of the LORD thy God," *tishma',* Qal [active] imperfect of *shawma'* = ***If you will begin to pay attention to the...*** *b^{a}qowl,* **call** "to keep his commandments" *lishmor,* Qal [active] infinitive construct of *shawmar'* = ***to attend to His...****mitsyah',* ***appointments...*** "and his statutes which are written in this book of the law, and if thou turn unto the LORD thy God" *taashuwb,* Qal [active] perfect of *shoob* = ***and return to your roots...*** "with all thine heart, and with all thy soul", *b^{a}kaal l^{a}baabkaa,* ***with the totality of your inner vehicle of love,*** *uwbkaal napshekaa,* ***and the totality of your*** nephesh, ***vital essence...***

211 Deuteronomy 30:6b "that thou mayest live" *lama'an,* ***for the purpose of...*** *chayeekaa,* ***retaining your freshness, vitality as in the wild...***

212 Romans 10:6 To reiterate: "Who shall ascend into heaven?" *Tis, Who? anabeesetai,* future middle of *anabaino* = *might have the ability, for his own sake to walk up...* [*ana* = up, *baino* = to pace] *eis ton ouranon, into the sky, eternity.*

213 Deuteronomy.30:11, "For this commandment which I command thee this day," *matsawakaa,* Piel participle of *tsawvaw'* = ***I am appointing the...****mitsveh,* ***edict...*** "it is not hidden from thee," *lo-nipleet,* Niphal participle of *pawlaw'* = ***it is not*** separated from you, being out of the ordinary, not extraordinary, not ***beyond the bounds of human powers or expectations...***"neither is it far off." *Walo' rachoqaah,* and in conjunction, ***it is not remote,*** receding. Deuteronomy 30:12 "It is not in heaven, that thou shouldest say," *lee'mor,* Qal [active] infinitive construct of *awmar'*= ***that you should suppose...*** "Who shall go up for us to heaven," *yaaleh,* Qal [active] imperfect of *awlah'* = ***Who can begin to make the ascent for us into the...****shawmah'yim,* sky, celestial, ***great unknown...*** "and bring it unto us, that we may hear it, and do it?", *w^{a}yashmi eenuw,* Hiphil (causative) imperfect of *shawmah'* = ***that we can begin to listen to it[self] and do it...*** *w^{a}na'asenaah,* Qal imperfect of *awsaw'* = ***to make something happen.***

the gap between His all-knowing nature and our limited, earth-bound perspective. He has bridged this gap by seeing to it that His appointment for our lives (His transcendent call) is "second nature" to us.

Mission: Impossible,[214] Romans 10:7, Deuteronomy 30:13. We are well aware of our limitations as humans, but Moses points out the most embarrassing limitation of man in this regard. The most condemning attribute of man is that, even if he was able to transcend these barriers, he does not care enough to make the effort required to retrieve his fellow man from exile. Moses indicates that God is different from man in both respects. God is able. He can transcend even the chasm of death, and He cares enough about us to make that journey. This kind of ability and this kind of care could not be understood by man until it was demonstrated by Jesus.[215] The reason for the necessity for transcending these abysses is unclear in Deuteronomy 30, so Paul adds in Romans 10:7 the needed parenthetical phrase adding purpose to the Deuteronomy passage: that is, "to bring Christ again from the dead".[216] If God has the ability and care to retrieve Christ from the dead (thereby demonstrating His ability to us), He has the capacity to retrieve us from the dead or from any other place of exile. The question is, who is able and has enough care for us and our "mortality worries" to bring the *corpus Christi* back from the other side of the sea, or from the bottom of the sea, or from the heavens, or out

214 *Mission: Impossible*. 1966-1973, 1988-1990. Created and produced by Bruce Geller. CBS Television Network.

215 Deuteronomy 30:13 "Neither is it beyond the sea" *mee'ber*, ***on the other side***, trans.., *yawm*, ***of the roar [of the surf]***, "that thou shouldest say, Who will go over the sea for us", *ya^abaar*, Qal [active] imperfect of *awbar* = ***who has the will to begin to cross over...***, *laanuw*, emphatic, ***and would care that much about us***, eleeber haayaam, ***[to go] over on the far side, across the billows...*** "and bring it unto us," *w^ayiqaachehaa*, Qal [active] imperfect of *lawkakh* = ***and begin to draw it back to us...*** "that we may hear it, and do it?", *w^ayashmi eenuw*, Hiphil (causative) imperfect of *shawmah'* = ***that we can begin to listen to it[self] and do it...*** *w^ana'asenaah*, Qal imperfect of *awsaw'* = ***to make something happen.***

216 Romans 10:7b "that is to bring Christ again from the dead" *tout*, ***for the intent that...****estin*, present indicative of *eime* = ***it now exists as...****Christou*, ***the anointed one, the Messiah...****ek nekron*, ***out of the necrotic, corpse***, disappearance... *anagagein*, aorist infinitive of *anago* = ***to lead up.*** [*ana* = up, *ago* = to lead].

of necrosis, or wherever it may have gone? We would be comforted about that ultimate barrier, death, if we could get more and better evidence about what happened to Christ in the resurrection and beyond. We have some questions we would like to ask Him in the flesh. We would like to know why Christ's body (why not just His soul?) had to be resurrected, why that body was different from the one He had when He walked on the water in Galilee, why it stayed around for fifty days, and where it is now. The more basic questions implied by Paul are: who has the ability to conjure up how Christ resurrected, and who can transcend the barrier of death by duplicating this great feat? To us, Christ seems far away, at least 2000 years away and separated from us by a deep, mysterious pit. These questions are all answered in Romans 10 as Paul amplifies Deuteronomy 30 and Isaiah 28.

The New Deal, Romans 10:8-11, Deuteronomy 30:14[217]

"I pledge you, I pledge myself, to a new deal for the American people."
Franklin Delano Roosevelt, July 2, 1932.

Pay Me Now or Pay Me Later, [218] **Romans 10:8-9a, Deuteronomy 30:14.** The answers to these questions seem beyond our reach. It seems to us that we can't even contemplate them at a peripheral level. The truth is that we are only a heartbeat away from eternity. Paul drives the point home that time and space, as Einstein reiterated later, are relative to the perspective of the one experiencing events. Paul, as was his wont, played

217 Romans 10: "8 But what saith it? The word is nigh thee, even in thy mouth, and in thy heart: that is, the word of faith, which we preach; 9 That if thou shalt confess with thy mouth the Lord Jesus, and shalt believe in thine heart that God hath raised him from the dead, thou shalt be saved. 10 For with the heart man believeth unto righteousness; and with the mouth confession is made unto salvation. 11 For the scripture saith, Whosoever believeth on him shall not be ashamed." Deuteronomy 30: "14 But the word is very nigh unto thee, in thy mouth, and in thy heart, that thou mayest do it."

218 "You can pay me now, or pay me later" the marketing slogan of The Fram Corporation now owned by Rank Group Ltd, Graeme Hart's private investment company.

on words to bring to our minds Isaiah's commentary on our bad deal with mortality. The play is with the phrase "the word is nigh thee". The literal translation of the Greek is "the stream of thought is squeezing near and is on the verge of inundating you, leaving you no place to hide".[219] Now, where have we heard something like that before? We remember Isaiah 28:17b: "and the waters shall overflow the hiding place".[220] The literal translation of that Hebrew passage is "the stream will be freed to inundate you revealing your secret". We are as close to Christ as the Bible and the story of His sacrifice and resurrection. That story (stream of thought) puts us in proximity with eternity. It is as close to us, and as real to us, as our tangible, physical existence.[221] The answer to our quest for eternity is so close to us that it is in our speech. Paul says that the story of Christ's victory over death is so intimately entwined with our nature that it pervades our intangible motivation; it is in our heart.[222] We know the truth when we hear it, because we feel at home in it, like it has always been a part of us; we feel it in our hearts (our cores). So, what is the truth, the stream that is so close to us as to be at the edge of our consciousness? It is very simple, maybe too simple. It is that there is only one way to prevent death from drowning us in the shame of our revealed bad deal with mortality. That only way is through trust in Christ that He will lead us through the valley

---

219 Romans 10:8 to reiterate: "But what saith it?" *alla'*, to the contrary, *ti, what? Leggei,* present indicative of *lego* = does it allege, is the idea laid forth... "the word is nigh thee" *engus,* it is squeezing near, threatening you with anguish, emphatic [*en* = in, *guion* = hand] on the verge, English = anxious, anguish...*sou, you...to rheema,* the stream of thought... [from *rheo* = to flow]...*estin,* present indicative of *eimi* = continuing to exist.

220 Isaiah 28:17b: "and the waters shall overflow the hiding place" *yshTaduw,* Qal [active] imperfect of *shawtaf* = the flood will be freed to inundate...*w^{a}ceeter,* the secret you thought you had gotten away with.

221 Romans 10:8a, "even in thy mouth" *en too stomata sou,* ***in your openings,*** stomates, referring to Deuteronomy 30:14: "But the word is very nigh unto thee" *qarowb,* **contiguous...***eeleykaa,* ***and continuous, near you...****dawbaw',* ***is the word...****maod,* ***also quickly...*** "in thy mouth", *batiykaa,* ***in your speech...***

222 Romans 10:8b, "in thy heart" *kai en tee kardia sou,* ***and in your core...,*** referring to Deuteronomy 30:14: *laybawb,* in your heart, used as "take heart" that is, in your motivation.

of the shadow of death.[223] We can prevent the inundating shame that occurs when death reveals our poor deal with mortality if we will yield to the flood of the revelation that God has taken care of our problem with mortality through His placement of the Cornerstone.[224] So, to our disappointment, nothing big is required of us. We don't need to earn a required number of merit badges to get to our truth, no long pilgrimage, no climbing of mountains, no running of marathons or obstacle courses; no tortuous journeys to Tibet are required to get the truth of the gospel. If we just sit still and listen, it will come to us: it is in our character; we feel it in our bones. All we have to do is vent our confidence in God and this will take the edge off the Edge.[225]

Don't Tell My Heart,[226] Romans 10:9-11. Paul says in Romans 10:9 that we must have integrity; the speech of our mouths must be consistent with what is in our hearts. All we have to say is what is in our hearts: that the Rock is personal to us, that the Rock has rocked our being, that we have confidence in Him as our Author and our Authority.[227] But, what

223 Psalm 23: "1 The LORD is my shepherd; I shall not want. 2 He maketh me to lie down in green pastures: he leadeth me beside the still waters. 3 He restoreth my soul: he leadeth me in the paths of righteousness for his name's sake. 4 Yea, though I walk through the valley of the shadow of death, I will fear no evil: for thou art with me; thy rod and thy staff they comfort me."

224 Romans 10:8, "that is" *tout*, that thing: that word, ***that [stream of ideas]...****estin*, present indicative of *eimi* = ***continues to exist as...*** "the word of faith, which we preach", *rheema*, ***the flow of the stream...****tees pisteos*, ***the confidence***, trust ***that...*** *kerussomen*, present indicative of *karusso* = ***we continue to herald...***

225 Romans 10:9a, "that" *hoti*, ***the substance [of your confidence that cannot be sensed]...*** "if thou shalt confess" *hean*, ***given the condition that...****homologeesees*, aorist subjunctive active of *homologeo* = ***you might say the same thing as [your core is crying out]...*** "with thy mouth" *en too stomata*, ***in the stomates, openings...****sou*, ***of you...*** "the Lord Jesus" *Kurion*, ***the author, owner...****Ieesous*, ***[whose name means] Jehovah saves...***

226 *Don't Tell My Heart*, 1991, written by Don Von Tress, recorded by Marcy Brothers, Renamed *Achy Breaky Heart*, 1992, recorded by Billy Ray Cyrus, album *Some Gave All*.

227 Romans 10:9b, "and shalt believe in thine heart" *kai*, ***in addition to [what your mouth says]...****pisteusees*, aorist subjunctive active of *pisteuo* = ***you might possibly have confidence, be willing to confide in [God]...****en tee kardia sou*, ***in the core of you.***

exactly must we have confidence in concerning God? Paul is explicit and answers this question in context of Isaiah 28:16 that he will quote again in vs. 11. In Romans 10:9b, he says that we must have confidence that God awakened Christ from the dead.[228] Because the soul is intangible (can only be sensed indirectly), God could not demonstrate to us that He has the power to cause the soul to live perpetually, but He could demonstrate that He has the power to cause the tangible body animated by the intangible soul to be resurrected. So, if we can believe God at this level (that He awakened Christ from the dead), it is no stretch to believe that God is also able to awaken us out of our necropsy. We can be free from our anxiety about death and be free of the tax that we pay in relation to our contract with mortality.[229] Our mortality ceases to matter to us since death is not a period that ends our lives, but is only a comma between our life here and our life there. We are thus liberated to live a sane life, free from the fears inherent in our mortal condition. Paul, in Romans 10:10, further characterizes the physical, spiritual connection that brings concept to reality.[230] Concept is abstract. Unless a tangible event verifying the concept occurs, the concept exists only in our minds (which may be good enough to qualify it as reality?). Righteousness

---

228 Romans 10:9c "that God has raised him from the dead" *hoti*, ***that [the substance of your confidence is...]*** *ho Theos*, ***the God...****auton*, ***him [Jesus]...****eegeiren*, aorist indicative active of *egeiro* = ***has, no doubt, at a specific time in history, aroused, awakened...****ek nekron*, ***out of the necropsy, the corpse...***

229 Romans 10:9d "thou shalt be saved", *sootheesee*, future passive of *sozo* = ***you will be protected [from the contract you have made with necropsy], delivered [from the flood of death]*** Latin: *salvo, libero, sanus*, English: be liberated to sanity.

230 Romans 10:10 "for with the heart" *gar*, ***the basis [for the heart-mouth axis being fundamental to your protection from the Covenant with Death]...****kardia*, ***[is that your] core...*** [Latin: *cor*, English: coronary, core]... "man believeth" *pisteuetei*, present indicative passive of *pisteuo* = ***has, no doubt, been endowed with confidence***, trust...*eis*, ***[that turns] into...****dikaiosuneen*, equity, justification, ***right relatedness*** [from *deiknuo*, to be thought of/exhibited as {a son having an inheritance}]... "and with the mouth" *de*, ***moreover, the bottom line is...****stomata*, ***the opening [through which is revealed what is within]...*** "confession is made" *homologeitai*, present indicative passive of *homologeo* = [forced to go along with the core] ***proclaims the same*** [*homo*] ***story*** [*logo*]... "unto salvation" *sooteerian*, ***into your rescue/safety [from the Covenant with Death]***.

was a concept until Jesus lived it out. He demonstrated that right living arises from right relatedness to God (We can become right-related only through adoption[231]). Right relatedness involves all the birthrights and privileges of being "family" including inheritance (an equity position). Paul says we gain this right relatedness through confidence in God, securing us from our Covenant with Death, releasing us to the potential of living as a pioneer blazing new trails on the frontier (the Edge) of our life on earth (Romans 10:11).

231 Romans 8:14-17:"14 For as many as are led by the Spirit of God, they are the sons of God. 15 For ye have not received the spirit of bondage again to fear; but ye have received the Spirit of adoption, whereby we cry, Abba, Father. 16 The Spirit itself beareth witness with our spirit, that we are the children of God: 17 And if children, then heirs; heirs of God, and joint-heirs with Christ; if so be that we suffer with him, that we may be also glorified together."

CHAPTER 5

PIONEER LIVING: ON BOTH SIDES OF THE EDGE

The Rock of Ages, John 14:1-2[232]

"While I draw this fleeting breath,
When mine eyes shall close in death,
When I soar to worlds unknown,
See thee on thy judgment throne,
Rock of Ages, cleft for me,
Let me hide myself in thee."

> *Rock of Ages, Gospel Magazine,* 1775, Augustus Montague Toplady.

Let's Hear it From the Rock, John 13, 14. The crisis had arrived for Jesus and His disciples. The stage was set. The pivotal night of their lives had arrived. In this fateful evening, Jesus would gather His disciples in the upper room, eat a memorial meal associated with the Passover festival, bid farewell to His betrayer, instigate His own memorial supper,

232 John 14: "1 Let not your heart be troubled: ye believe in God, believe also in me. 2 In my Father's house are many mansions: if it were not so, I would have told you. I go to prepare a place for you. 3 And if I go and prepare a place for you, I will come again, and receive you unto myself; that where I am, there ye may be also."

and teach His intimate inner circle one last, unforgettable lesson. [233] Since Jesus knew that He was on the brink of eternity and that this would be His last teaching this side of the grave, His subject matter possibly deserves even more attention than that of His other teachings.[234] Later in the evening, as He continued His teaching, He would leave the upper room, and walk with His disciples into the night. He would lead His disciples to the relative seclusion of the Garden of Gethsemane on the Mount of Olives. In the Garden, He would pray, be betrayed, be arrested, and be taken to His trials before the Jewish Sanhedrin and the hierarchy of local Roman officials. The next day, He would be beaten and crucified (or should we say tortured to death). Jesus had made it plain to His disciples that this Passover would be like no other in its millennium of history.

A House of Cards, John 13, 14. It was apparent to Jesus' disciples that, through Jesus' unwavering determination to participate in this Passover, He was purposefully exposing Himself to His enemies in the Jewish authoritative body, the Sanhedrin. His enemies feared that He might precipitate a riot in the large crowd (perhaps two million visitors) that had gathered in Jerusalem for the festival. The Sanhedrin had a codependent relationship with the Roman Procurator, Pontius Pilate. The Procurator appointed the high priest as the chief of the Sanhedrin who had oversight of the temple and thus the religion of the Jews. The high priest controlled the temple complex and had the authority to collect its lucrative taxes. In turn, the Sanhedrin kept the peace among the restless native population who detested their Roman overseers and their puppet government. Pilate felt his position to be precarious with the emperor in Rome because he had acted several times in ways that infuriated the Jews to the extent that the resulting riots were large enough to cause vibrations to be felt in

---

233 *The Harmony of the Gospels*, 1932, A.T. Robertson, HarperCollins Publishing, ISBN 0060668903.

234 John 13:1 "Now before the Feast of the Passover, when Jesus knew that his hour was come that he should depart out of this world unto the Father, having loved his own which were in the world, he loved them unto the end."

Rome.[235] Thus, Caesar already was suspicious that Pilate was a marginal administrator of limited abilities to keep the *Pax Romana* [236] in this troublesome corner of the empire. Pilate could ill afford another event of proportions large enough to reach the ears of Rome. The position of Procurator had become precarious in recent years; Pilate knew that one more perceived failure to control the unruly populace would cause him to be removed from power as four of his immediate predecessors had been removed. So, if Jesus precipitated a riot, a series of sequential events might bring down the whole precarious arrangement as actually did happen about 35 years later when the Romans finally brutally squelched the Jewish rebellion in A.D. 70.[237] The disciples did not know whether the Romans would arrest Jesus on that particular night, but they were prepared for a fight. At least, some of them were armed (Luke 22:38). Peter spoke for the group, pledging that they would be willing to go all the way with Jesus (John 13:37). Jesus' reply both perplexed them and

---

235 Pilate "was the fifth Roman procurator of Judaea, his predecessors having been Coponius, Marcus Ambivulus, Annius Rufus, and Valerius Gratus. Pilate had held the office for ten years during the reign of Tiberius. His arbitrary conduct in introducing Caesar's ensigns into Jerusalem, and in bringing water into the city for which he paid with money belonging to the Temple, led to successive risings amongst his subjects (Jos. "Ant." and "Wars"). Philo accuses him of 'bribery, violence, robbery, cruelty, insult, continual executions without semblance of justice, endless and unendurable atrocities.' If this, perhaps, as the testimony of an enemy is too strong, it is certain that Pilate was a Roman governor of the regulation type, who acted without the slightest regard for the peculiarities (especially religious) of the provinces over which he ruled, and punished every opposition to his arbitrary conduct with the greatest severity. It would not be easy to find another man so well fitted to drive the Jewish nation to desperation. Accused before Vitellius, the preces of Syria, he was deposed, and sent to Rome to answer for his administration." T. Whitelaw, D. D., *The Biblical Illustrator*, Nashville, TN, ISSN 0195-1351,from The *Biblical Illustrator* Copyright © 2002, 2003 Ages Software, Inc. and Biblesoft, Inc.

236 The burden of the government to keep the peace, The History of the Decline and Fall of the Roman Empire, 1776-1777, Edward Gibbon, Everyman Publishing, ISBN 9781857150957.

237 These dynamics are vividly described by the contemporary historian, Titus Flavius Josephus in *The Wars of the Jews*, A.D.75, and in *Antiquities of the Jews*, A.D. 94.

gave a perspective on life that was new to the disciples and new to us. He expanded on a theme familiar to the disciples, the theme Paul elaborated on in his *remez* (Romans 9:33-10:11) on the Covenant with Death, the theme of life as a journey. As Paul said in Romans, life is a journey requiring the journeyman to deal with death one way or the other. Jesus elaborated on this old picture with the clarification embedded in the revolutionary twist that changed everything. That twist was introduced in the long ago by the author of Isaiah 28:16, the twist of the mysterious Cornerstone.

From Here to Eternity,[238] **John 14:1a.** Jesus begins His allusion (*remez*) in response to Peter's apparent failure to keep abreast of current events. Peter was on shaky ground when he made the promise (boast?), "I will lay down my life for thy sake" (John 13:37). Although Jesus replied to Peter in John 14:1-4, He was also addressing all men who live on the brink, journeying under the banner of their Covenant with Death. In the first statement of His *remez*, Jesus put forth **five** surprising assumptions. The **first** assumption is that the "steady state" of our hearts is trouble. The disciples had every reason to be unsettled by the fast moving, disturbing events unfolding on this fateful night when their rabbi was on the verge of being arrested. They feared that they would be included in the Roman search for the guilty. They too might be arrested and led away to be crucified along with their presumed ringleader. But, the basal assumption that Jesus made is that all men everywhere, not just the disciples on this particular night, are continually in the process of being stirred up and in turmoil. This "steady state", as we have seen, arises from the continuing tax we pay for the private deal we have made with our mortality. We carry at least a subliminal level of chronic disturbance because we cannot shake the fact that our "lease on life" is only a lease. As far as the disciples were concerned, they could have been imminently facing eternity on that

238 *From Here to Eternity*, 1953, novel written by James Joyce, film based on the novel directed by Fred Zimmermann, starring Burt Lancaster, Montgomery Clift, Frank Sinatra, Deborah Kerr.

fateful night. In a less dramatic way, each of us could be facing eternity at any time. At least that possibility underpins our subconsciousness.

Only You Can Prevent Forest Fires, [239] **John 14:1a.** The **second** assumption is in a word not stated but implicitly implied. That word is "you". Jesus' assumption is that <u>you</u> can control your *cardia*.[240] You can prevent your core from being troubled. Only you can prevent a core meltdown. Only you can alter your deal with death and avoid the accompanying tax. The irony is that it is you that got you in this mess to start with and it is only God that can get you out. Your role in escaping the deal, as we have seen, is to make the decision as to whom you will trust in terms of how to handle the problem of continually living on the brink. If you trust yourself, you are doomed to continual payment of the death tax and your *cardia* is chronically destabilized. Jesus did not say we can prevent ourselves from experiencing trouble, but He did say that we can avoid being continually troubled at the core. Having trouble does not necessarily lead to being troubled. We have a way of escaping the seeming inevitable connection between having trouble and being troubled. Jesus' reply to Peter hit home to our problem with death and with our Covenant with Death.

The Big League, John 14:1

"It Ain't Over 'Til It's Over"
Yogi Berra, *circa* 1980.

In Over Our Heads, John 14:1a. The **third** assumption is in the picture painted by the term "be troubled". As Isaiah 28 indicates, when the chips are down, we have to admit that we are "out of our depth". Jesus' last teaching before His crucifixion began with an image reminiscent of the inundating flood image of Isaiah 8:7 and 28:17: "when the overflowing

---

239 "Only You Can Prevent Forest Fires", 1947, slogan of Smokey the Bear of the U.S. Forest Service created by the Ad Council.

240 John 14:1a, "Let not your heart" *meh,* ***possibly not...*** *humōn hee,* ***your...*** *kardia,* heart, Latin: *cor,* English: ***core***.

scourge shall pass through, then ye shall be trodden down by it." That image is embodied in the Greek verb translated as "troubled".[241] This word paints the picture from Isaiah 28 of a river-bottom farmer caught in the storm waters and the resulting rising flood. The source of the flood, of course, is also the source of his good times, the river. The river is now hardly recognizable. It has run amok, overflowing its banks. Those caught in the flood are subject to panic as they confront their destiny when they are suddenly submerged into the rapidly moving, deep torrent. We cannot swim well enough to save ourselves from this drowning, but we still play a role in our salvation because it is up to us to submit to a capable, trustworthy lifeguard.

Off in a Storm, John 14:1a. Another similarly vivid picture painted by the word "troubled" is of a sailor who is on board the relative safety of a ship in the storm-plagued Mediterranean Sea as was the case for Paul off the island of Malta.[242] Before the sailor can prepare himself, a sudden storm blows up from nowhere; the wind rises to gale force; the waves lap over the deck of the suddenly-vulnerable ship. To the sailor's horror, the ship takes on water and then sinks with alarming swiftness, leaving him gurgling under the cold water in high seas. He has no life preserver and finds himself alone in the open water. He is floundering, tossed by the sea, having no foundation. The frantic, shipwrecked sailor is intimidated by being thrust abruptly into the expanse of the sea with no land in sight and with his unexpected confrontation with the proximity of his death, He sees no shoreline; he knows that he can swim only a short time in the turbulent seas; he has already swallowed some salt water. He is shaken to the core. Panic precipitates drowning. This picture fits our state of

241 John 14:1. "be troubled", *terasesthoo*, present imperative of *terasso* = ***[don't] continue to be stirred up***, agitated, anxious, vulnerable, worried, a picture of a person out of his depth, off in a storm, tossed about without foundations as by the sea, who has lost his moorings, the basic state of turmoil and turbulence [Latin, *terror*].

242 Acts 27:40-44. The Mediterranean Sea is known for its winter storms. *Cleopatra, A Life*, 2010, Stacy Schiff, 2010. Back Bay Books, Little Brown and Company, New York, NY, ISBN 978-0-316-00192-2.

mind when we are forced to confront the great expanse of eternity. We flounder about, looking for any port in the storm, settling for the only lifesaver we can find, our poor deal with mortality. But, Jesus is offering another way, a way for us to take charge of our destiny, to take charge of the status of our hearts. We don't have to flail about desperately trying to keep our noses above the water. The implication is that we can take control of our hearts and live boldly. So, how do we accomplish this? What must we do?

California is a Brand New Game,[243] John 14:1b. We develop our Covenant with Death because we find it necessary to throw up a smoke screen of confidence based on faith that we can handle our mortal condition. As Isaiah 28 demonstrates, this confidence is tragically misplaced. (Misplaced trust appears as arrogance.) As Isaiah said, this kind of faith is actually based on a lie we sell ourselves. As we have seen, the truth is that our insecurity (troubled heart) actually gives us a poor platform for handling our mortal condition. Jesus says that the key for escaping our Covenant with Death and the associated death tax is confidence but, as I have noted, not self-confidence. Jesus' **fourth** assumption at the beginning of His *remez* is that once we face the music that we have made a bad deal by trusting in ourselves, we have only one other option. Given the status of our desperation for any port in the storm and the imminent, inundating flood, the only other option to believing in ourselves is to "believe in God".[244] Some may claim to have no belief in God, but few can maintain this posture when they confront imminent death. But the relevant question remains: Is this enough? Is faith in God alone satisfactory qualification for saving us from our bad deal with mortality? Not according to Jesus. His **fifth** assumption is

243 "It don't matter at all where you've played before, California's a brand new game." *All the Gold in California,* 1998, sung by Larry Gatlin and the Gatlin Brothers, album *Larry Gatlin and the Gatlin Brothers Super Hits.*

244 John 14: 1 "Ye believe in God", *pisteuete,* present indicative active of *pisteuo* = ***There is now no doubt that you continue to be convinced…****eis ton Theon,* ***into the God.***

that we must not only have confidence in God, but we must also have faith in Him.[245] This is the only task that must be accomplished in order to enable us to take control of our hearts. This trust in Jesus will allow us to live boldly, discarding the shackles endemic in our mortality problem. This is our only avenue for escape from the inundating flood that threatens to destroy the elaborate scheme we so carefully constructed in our Covenant with Death. We might have thought that dealing with the "afterlife" is like dealing with our present life, and it is in a way. But, when we contemplate that afterlife deal, we must confront the stark reality that it is, in some ways, a brand new game. We can't have much self-confidence in "playing" that game because the rules may be different from any game we have played before. The only thing we know for sure is that if we don't trust Jesus in this life we will not have the confidence required for us to get beyond the Edge to continue our journey on the other side.

Confidence Defined: Daddy's Hands,[246] John 14:1b. I was nine years old when the great "time it never rained"[247] drought broke in 1956. The wheat crop next to our house was golden in its ripeness and almost chest high. A combine sat in the edge of the field waiting for the moisture in the grain to drop just a little more. On that hot, still, muggy June day, as dusk arrived, I had fed the chickens and was returning to our screened in back porch when I noticed in the northwest, a deepening ominous gloom caused by towering storm clouds. The blackness of the advancing battle line was soon punctuated with brilliant flashes accompanied with rolling thunder. The war was announced by the sudden arrival of a brisk wind carrying the distinctive pungent odor of impending rain, usually a pleasant experience, but not this time. This time, the storm struck so quickly that we were blindsided by its violent fury. This time, in the sudden pitch darkness, my

245 John 14:1 "believe also in me" *kai eis eme,* ***in conjunction [with your confidence in God], into me*** [emphatic]...*pisteuete,* present imperative of *pisteuo,* ***you must have confidence.***

246 *Daddy's Hands,* 1986, written and sung by Holly Dunn.

247 *The Time it Never Rained,* 1973, Elmer Kelton, Doubleday, New York, NY, ISBN 0-385-05075-5.

mother Naomi, daddy Joe, sister Sue and I, flashlights in hand, braved the horizontal cold rain to make the 100 yard dash across the farmyard to the storm cellar. We descended the concrete stairs and sat on the musty mattress in the light of a kerosene lantern giving the illusion of calmness to the dungeon we called a cellar. This illusion was eradicated by the roaring gale attacking the cellar door requiring our collective weight on the rope attached to the door to prevent it from being ripped away, exposing us to the torrent. After an age of time, the storm abated tempting us to venture out to see what we had to see. Daddy put me on his shoulders, and my mother carried Sue as we sloshed across the lake that had magically appeared between the cellar and the house. A sudden latent lightning flash defiantly reached out of the receding storm to illuminate what had been the wheat field. Nothing was in the field except lakes that stretched between the terraces which were populated with dead jackrabbits that had been killed by softball sized hailstones that remained floating in the water. These chunks of ice had also beaten off the shingles and crashed through the windows of our frame house; the sheetrock had fallen in on our soggy beds, and the floors were covered with water and debris. That event changed our lives. We sold that flooded out, droughty farm and moved to another that had poorer soil but was free of emotional baggage. The overriding emotion cascading from that event that influenced me most, however, is the incongruent warmth that I felt from an emerging confidence in my daddy and my family, that we would find a way to make it through the storm and its devastation. That event provided the contrast required for me to see that my family was about love, about survival in the face of catastrophe, and about me being a part of it all. When the storm passes over and the flood hits our door, we need to have a guide that we can confide in, that we can have confidence in to carry us through. I was confident in the future because I was confident in my family that through thick and thin we would stick together, that we belonged to each other and that we could trust in our union above even catastrophic events. This incident in my life gave depth to an old adage; confidence is a matter of knowing in your heart that you belong.

The Son of the Pioneer, John 14:2

"The cowpokes loped on past him and he heard one call his name,
If you want to save your soul from hell a-riding on our range,
Then cowboy, change your ways today, or with us you will ride,
A-trying to catch the devil's herd across these endless skies."

(Ghost) Riders in the Sky: A Cowboy Legend, 1948, written by Stan Jones, sung by Sons of the Pioneers.

Home Boy, John 14:2. So, the question is: What is so special about Jesus that qualifies Him as being worthy of our confidence? Jesus gives us **three** characteristics that make Him imminently and uniquely qualified for the job as guide. Jesus indicates that He is worthy of our confidence because of His unique credentials. His **first** qualification is associated with His unique experience base. He knows the other side of the grave as well as He knows this side. As stated by Paul in Romans 14:9, Jesus has experience and dominion in both domains: the living and the dead.[248] He is the only one in all history who came to earth from God, who died, and afterward lived to tell of it. In John 14:2, Jesus speaks with familiarity of His Father's residence, both the physical and the spiritual.[249] Jesus is very familiar with His Patron, they go way back (John 1:1 "In the beginning was the word..."). So Jesus is well aware of the home place of the family and therefore can serve as the only qualified guide beyond the Edge to that fair land.[250]

---

248 Romans 14:9. "For to this end Christ both died, and rose, and revived, that he might be Lord both of the dead and living."

249 John 14:2 "In my Father's house" *en tee oikia, **in the residence**,* household, family, abode, the physical and spiritual universe as the greater domain, the temple in Jerusalem as the specific domain...*tou Patros, **of the Paternal one***, the one who patronizes, is the progenitor.

250 John 14:2 "are many mansions" *monai pollai eisen: eisen,* present indicative of *eimi* = ***there continues to exist...**pollai,* ***an abundant number...**monai,* ***of stations on a journey**,* quarters for the night, resting places, oases in the desert [from *mone*, a staying as in monastery, from *meno*, to dwell as in menopause: the pause that dwells, Vulgate: *mansiones*, related to *monos*, the habitat of the one, you].

The Truth Hurts, John 14:2. The **second** credential that makes Jesus imminently trustworthy as the guide to the "mansion land" is His trait of being brutally honest. He tells His disciples in vs. 2, "if it were not so, I would have told you".[251] To prevent the traveler from being surprised in his travels, it is necessary that the guide not keep anything from the traveler. One might imagine instances in travel where the guide might want to "protect" the traveler by holding back certain information, especially if the news might cause the traveler to worry. The gospels quote Jesus as saying many things that were not sugarcoated. We would like to have had the opportunity to edit some of these sayings to make them more palatable, more politically correct, possibly less stark and offensive to certain groups. Jesus taught us that oftentimes the truth hurts. One example will suffice; Jesus said that it is easier for a camel to go through the eye of a needle than for a rich man to enter heaven.[252] Fortunately, for our good in the present instance, Jesus can be trusted to be consistent with His reputation of always being brutally honest. He never withheld from us the naked truth, no matter how much it might hurt us. So, in this instance, we know He is being true to Himself. But, fortunately for us, this time the truth is music to our ears. Jesus says that if it had been set up by a capricious god that the destiny of life for all was to be calamity, He would not have protected us by withholding the information, the sad news. Instead, Jesus says that, if this had been the case, He would not have permitted us to indulge in vain hope concerning future blessedness. He always tells us the truth, the whole truth and nothing but the truth – even if it hurts. Therefore, Jesus' statement on the eve of His death that the (head) stone is only a milestone in a continuing journey carries much force and credibility. Before Dr. Joe Whiteman took on the task of teaching farm boys how to search for the truth in the Animal Science Department of Oklahoma State University, he was a World War II era

---

251 John 14:2 "if it were not so, I would have told you."*ei*, ***given the case that...****de*, ***the bottom line had been...****meh*, ***of the possibility to the contrary...****eipon*, aorist indicative active of *epo* = ***I would, no doubt, have spoken up...****an*, **about my suspicion...***humin*, ***to you...***

252 Matthew 19:24; Mark 10:25; Luke 18:25.

Marine Corps Drill Sergeant. He fit the part well: he was tall, lean, and had a gravelly voice that carried above all others. He had a presence that demanded respect (if not fear). I would not say that Dr. Whiteman took glee in explaining to us the error of our ways, but I will say the task did not bother him. Dr. Whiteman was a stickler for the truth and the inerrant pursuit of the truth. He did not tolerate sloppy work or any deviation that hindered that search. He could explain perceived failure in this regard in very direct, unyielding language that farm boys could understand. It was easy for graduate students to get "ahead of themselves" thinking that they were the best in the land, maybe even surpassing their teachers. One such student thought he had reached equivalence with Dr. Whiteman and, one day, addressed him as "Joe". Dr. Whiteman responded by looking the student in the eye and explaining that the student did not know him well enough to address him as "Joe". I still call him Dr. Whiteman 35 years after the fact. As a graduate student, I had assisted Dr. Whiteman in teaching his senior level research methods course several times so I felt that I had an inside track to making an "A" in Dr. Whiteman's graduate level research methods course. Dr. Whiteman demonstrated to me that I knew a lot less than I thought I did by rewarding my efforts with a "B". He was right, of course, but I still did not want to hear it. For our good, someone needs to be willing to tell us the stark truth, especially the truth concerning the grave.

Illustration 4, The Need to Know. Journeying can be dangerous; a good guide is necessary to navigate roads such as these in western China (left) and "the detour" in the Andes of Peru (right).

The Need to Know, John 14:2. I traveled with Dr. Jodi Sterle, an imminent swine scientist now at Iowa State University, to the high Andes of Peru to assist the cattle and swine enterprises of the orphanage/farm *Casa Del Aguila* (The House of the Eagle)[253] in the mountains about 100 miles from Cusco (elevation 11,600 feet). This mission, dedicated to retrieving Peruvian orphans from the precipice, is led by Steve Dyer and was founded by Ralph Fair (both from Texas) who guided us on this trip. We went during the rainy season, and it did rain - every night. I became a little concerned when the Urubamba River bordering the farm overflowed its banks, especially since our only road out crossed this river. I suggested that we leave quickly before the flood worsened. Mr. Fair said, "Not to worry; if all else fails, we can always go 'over the top'". I became a little more concerned when we heard that the railroad from Cusco to Machu Picchu had been washed away, stranding hundreds of tourists. Mr. Fair said, "Not to worry; if all else fails, we can always go 'over the top'". My concern deepened when the river covered the road. Mr. Fair said, "Not to worry; if all else fails, we can always go 'over the top'". Then, my concern matured when the river completely washed away the road. Mr. Fair said, "Not to worry; we <u>will</u> go 'over the top'". So, we set out in three trucks to go "over the top". One truck full of men left in the morning "to clear the road" and we left in the other two trucks in the afternoon. We learned much about going "over the top" as we went. (It was on a need to know basis.) We learned sequentially that: 1. The escape route was not a road but was only a trail used exclusively by locals living in the mountains traveling mostly by mule; 2. The rain had caused landslides, blocking this trail in many places; 3. The trail was generally not quite wide enough for a truck, and it followed the edge of the mountain along breathtaking precipices; 4. The trail was completely blocked by a stream and a serious landslide that could not be traversed by vehicle; 5. We were to wade across this stream and climb over the landslide, carrying our luggage, abandoning our trucks; 6. A pastor was making his way up the other side of the mountain in a truck and would pick us up to take us to Cusco; 7. The pastor was late,

253 www.DYERFAMILYMISSIONS.com, www.CTEN.org/stevedyer.

could not be reached by phone, and we had to carry our baggage for several miles on this trail, having faith that he was actually on his way to meet us; 8. When we finally met the pastor, he had driven up the trail from Cusco, but the trail was too narrow to turn his vehicle around; 9. We (all eight of us) had to ride in the bed of the truck while we backed down the narrow, steep trail until we found a spot wide enough to turn around; 10. This spot was so narrow, with so great a precipice, that our hearts raced as we turned around; 11. After we turned around, in looking back, we noticed that the rain had undercut the trail at that point, so that we had been suspended over a precipitous cliff; 12. The pastor was not taking us to Cusco but was taking us to a rendezvous spot (his church) where we would hire taxis to take us to Cusco; 13. And finally, we learned (and Jodi won't let me forget this lesson) that sometimes it is best to be kept in the dark when traveling; sometimes you do not want to know. But, Jesus said that He would have told us if our journey was to end in catastrophe. His credentials give Him the credibility to lead us "over the top" and beyond the Edge.

Both Sides Now,[254] **John 14:2.** The **third** credential qualifying Jesus as the necessary object of our confidence is His understanding of our humanity and His willingness to serve our need. His understanding of our humanity and His care for us is imbedded in the promise of vs. 2: "I go to prepare a place for you". The Greek word translated as "prepare" means to conform to fit the necessary requirements of the user, allowing comfort. Each of us has peculiarities causing the adage "one size does not fit all" to be universally true. Jesus knows each of our sizes and our peculiarities. He also knows the requirements allowing for a good fit.[255] Jesus lived the gritty existence of a carpenter in the

254 *Both Sides Now*, 1967, written and sung by Joni Mitchell, album *Clouds*, sung by Judy Collins, 1967, album *Wild Flowers*.

255 John 14:2 "I go to prepare a place for you" *hoti*, ***the reason [I am telling about your place to spend the night] is...****poreuomai*, present indicative middle of *poreuo* = ***I now, no doubt, will journey***/transport ***across the portal [death's door] for the purpose:...****hetoimasai*, aorist infinitive of *hetoimazo* = ***to make ready...*** [from heteos = fitness] a configuring to fit your needs of...*topon humin*, ***a spot***, habitation [English: topological, topographical] ***for occupancy by you...***

small country town of Nazareth and participated in the fishing ventures of the Galilean fishing company of Zebedee and Sons (Peter, Andrew, James, and John: Mark 1:17-20). Thus, we perceive that Jesus knows what it means to be human. We learn as we read of His interactions with men and women during His life that He understands, not only humanity, but each of us individually, even better than we understand ourselves. His interaction with the woman at the well comes to mind as an example of His insight into the human plight (John 4:6-17). As we have seen, He also is familiar with His Father's domain. Therefore, He knows how to make fit resting places for us in our journey into the unknown, even beyond the Edge.

The Final Frontier, John 14:2-6, Numbers 10:28-34.[256]

"The frontier created freedom, breaking the bonds of custom".

> *The Significance of the Frontier in American History*, 1893, Frederick Jackson Turner.

---

256 John 14: "2 In my Father's house are many mansions: if it were not so, I would have told you. I go to prepare a place for you. 3. And if I go and prepare a place for you, I will come again, and receive you unto myself; that where I am, there ye may be also. 4 And whither I go ye know, and the way ye know. 5 Thomas saith unto him, Lord, we know not whither thou goest; and how can we know the way? 6 Jesus saith unto him, I am the way, the truth, and the life: no man cometh unto the Father, but by me."
Numbers 10: "28 Thus were the journeyings of the children of Israel according to their armies, when they set forward. 29 And Moses said unto Hobab, the son of Raguel the Midianite, Moses' father in law, We are journeying unto the place of which the LORD said, I will give it you: come thou with us, and we will do thee good: for the LORD hath spoken good concerning Israel. 30 And he said unto him, I will not go; but I will depart to mine own land, and to my kindred. 31 And he said, Leave us not, I pray thee; forasmuch as thou knowest how we are to encamp in the wilderness, and thou mayest be to us instead of eyes. 32 And it shall be, if thou go with us, yea, it shall be, that what goodness the LORD shall do unto us, the same will we do unto thee. 33 And they departed from the mount of the LORD three days' journey: and the ark of the covenant of the LORD went before them in the three days' journey, to search out a resting place for them.34 And the cloud of the LORD was upon them by day, when they went out of the camp."

By the Flickering Firelight,[257] **John 14:2.** Jesus refers to the home place as having "many mansions".[258] The translation of *monai* as mansions is unfortunate, not only because it implies sedentary, luxurious accommodations, but also because it implies a static existence. The picture of a static existence on the other side of the grave is undermined by the fact that "many mansions" does not necessarily mean a mansion corresponding to each of us but may refer to many resting places for each of us. This static picture is also undercut by the possibility that the word translated as many (*pollai*) could mean many in sequence. This interpretation is consistent with the unfolding story of Jesus' *remez.* Even though our resting places might not fit our picture of mansions (e.g. Versailles, Biltmore), we know from the previous paragraph that we will feel at home in our resting places. The scout will see to it.

Frontier Travel, John 14:2-3. Jesus indicates that His purpose is not just to find and prepare camping spots for us, but also to "come again" (John 14:3). He says the signal giving assurance that He will return is His departure.[259] The nature of His return is peculiar since His departure is accomplished through His death. From our perspective, death looks like a dead end, and if not a dead end, a one-way portal to the unknown (Hades). So, if Jesus can actually fulfill this promise to return, He will prove that death is not as it appears. The purpose of His return as given

---

257 "In the misty moonlight, By the flickering firelight, Any place is all right, Long as I'm with you", *In the Misty Moonlight*, 1967, written by Cindy Walker, the most successful version was recorded and sung by Dean Martin.

258 To Reiterate: John 14:2 "are many mansions" *monai pollai eisen: eisen,* present indicative of *eimi* = there continues to exist...*pollai,* an abundant number... *monai,* of stations on a journey, quarters for the night, resting places, oases in the desert [from *mone,* a staying as in monastery, from *meno,* to dwell as in menopause: the pause that dwells, Vulgate: *mansiones,* related to *monos,* the habitat of the one-you].

259 John 14:3, "if I go to prepare a place for you," This is the same phrase as in vs. 2 with the preamble of *hean* (that is: *hean hoti poreuomai hetoimasei topon humin), **given the condition that I depart from you,..*** "I will come again" *palin,* ***repeatedly*** [from *pale'* = to vibrate, oscillatory repetition] ***to...****erchomai,* present indicative middle: ***come, as one personally arriving in a timely manner...***

in John 14:3 is to "receive you unto myself that where I am, there you may be also".[260] Jesus says that the purpose for Him returning and taking us alongside is not for us to be with our friends or loved ones but for us to be with Him. If we grow in familiarity with Him during our journey through this life at His leadership, we will become increasingly at-home with Him, so that the spot that is home to Him will be home to us, even if that spot is on the other side of the grave. Jesus has taken on the task of moving us out of "our comfort zone" into unfamiliar territory where we have never been and, by definition, where we have no reason to feel comfortable. It is easy to become complacent in our way of thinking and to fall back to familiar concepts that do not threaten our "house of cards". Journeys out to the Edge are frightening and undermine our settled position in the world. Unfortunate for our need to be secure, Jesus consistently in his teaching took us to the edge of our view of correct behavior. One example of many is his direction in the Sermon on the Mount for us to "love our enemies".[261] Even though moving on to new territory in the mind opens the opportunity for vulnerability (practicing love always creates vulnerability), living in the new space created is stimulating and exciting. This is true regardless of the dimension of travel that one takes. The first step is always to challenge our present concepts, thereby opening the opportunity to get beyond them. It is comforting to rest in good theories, but good theories can be obstacles to moving on to deeper levels of insight. When I arrived at the University of Tennessee as a relatively newly minted PhD, I felt I had the world of beef cattle production pretty well "down pat". There, I met a former World War II fighter pilot who

---

260 John 14:3, "and receive you unto myself that where I am, there you may be also" *paraleempsomai*, future middle of *paralambano* = ***to be thrilled to receive you near as an intimate act of familiarity, as a close friend you can be comfortable with...****pros emauton*, ***toward me in a personal way...****hina*, ***to the intent that... ****hopou*, ***at the spot where...****eimi ego*, present indicative, ***I no doubt exist...****kai humeis eeti*, present subjunctive of *eimi* = ***that also you might exist as well...***

261 Luke 6: "27 But I say unto you which hear, Love your enemies, do good to them which hate you," Matt 5: "44 But I say unto you, Love your enemies, bless them that curse you, do good to them that hate you, and pray for them which despitefully use you, and persecute you;"

was an old hand with taking mind risks. Dr. Will Butts explained to me that my "cut-and-dried" way of thinking about the subject was okay – as far as it went; I just had the wrong perspective. He explained that, in actuality a beef cow does not have nutrient requirements that must be met in the feed provided her (as I had thought); she actually carves out a niche for herself in her environment, and interacts with that niche to produce and reproduce. This new perspective caused me many sleepless nights but, in the end, created a new level of inspiration that led me on a very exciting journey that I would have missed except that I was forced to reevaluate my complacent way of thinking. If one does not want to be shaken from complacency, I would recommend that he not read the teachings of the great pioneer, Jesus. These teachings can move us out of our comfort zone but, in the end, we will find the trip exciting and that excitement will give us a new level of comfort; we will find a new home on the other side of the Edge.

Illustration 5, The Frontier Scout. All journeymen need resting places along the journey and a good guide to lead them to the resting places: oasis south of the Dead Sea from afar on left and near on right.

The Frontier Scout, Numbers 10:28-34. As we dwell on this passage of scripture in John 14, a picture gradually emerges. It is faint to begin with, but as we let the components sink in, the picture becomes distinct. It is a picture that is familiar with nearly everyone who has moved during their life. The pieces of the puzzle are: 1. Jesus is departing on a journey; 2. His journey has the purpose of finding and preparing a place that suits those He leaves but who will follow Him later; 3. this fitting place is one of many, possibly in the sequential sense; 4. He will return to rendezvous with those He left behind so He can welcome them into His fellowship; and 5. the picture painted presents the possibility that He will do this repeatedly. The only allegory that fits all aspects in the teaching is that of the wagon boss, the frontier scout guiding migrating frontier families traveling beyond the edge into the unknown. The picture painted in this promise Jesus made on that fateful night is derived from the custom of migrating families traveling into unknown territory. All through history, as people migrated into the unfamiliar, they would hire a scout/guide who was familiar with the frontier. (This is the basis of flourishing tour guide companies all over the world.) This scout would make forays out in front of the wagon train to look for potential problems, prepare the way, and search for places with water and possibly shelter so the slower-moving pioneering party would have suitable camping sites. When the scout discovered the right spot for the next encampment and had made certain that it fit the needs of the travelers, he would return to the wagon train to usher it to the camping spot. Because of the possibility of missing the sojourners as he returned to find them, the sight of the wagons was always a moment of joy and relief as was the sight of the scout to the travelers. Jesus is not just alluding to this generalized, though well recognized picture. He had reference to a specific incident (example of this picture) in the historical life of Israel, an incident with which His disciples had familiarity since it was recorded in Numbers 10:28-34.

On To the Promised Land, Numbers 10:28. Because we have all been on journeys, we can identify with the plight of Moses and the children of Israel as they journeyed from the mount of God (Mount Horeb, Exodus 18:5) on their way to the Promised Land.[262] Similarly, we can identify

262 Numbers 10:28 "Thus were the journeying of the children of Israel" *eeleh,* ***this chronicles the...****mac'eeh,* ***march from [Mount Horeb],*** where Moses saw the burning bush [Exodus 3:13], where the Lord promised the land and challenged them to journey [Deuteronomy 2-6] where God covenanted with them through the giving of the Ten Commandments [Exodus 24:12] *bªneey,* ***of the sons of...*** *Yisraeel,* ***the tribe known as: he will rule as God.***

with Paul's use of this motif to describe the course of our lives (Romans 9:30-32) as well as the extended journey beyond the grave depicted by Jesus' *remez* in John 14:1-6. This journey of the children of Israel was like the one described by Jesus in that it was across a seemingly impenetrable barrier requiring passage into the daunting unknown. This territory was the desert for Moses and is death for Jesus and for us.

Reckless Abandonment, Numbers 10:29-32

"Dance with the one that brung you"
Darrell Royal, *circa* 1960-70.

An Experienced Guide, Numbers 10:29, 31. Facing the necessity to journey through an intimidating unknown, the children of Israel made the expedient and practical decision historically made by most journeymen. They attempted to solicit the services of the best guide they could find, Hobab. Hobab certainly had credentials qualifying him for the job. His character held promise as indicated by a cursory look at his name. The Hebrew word for Hobab implied a desire to build strong, loving relationships.[263] His pedigree also indicated possibilities. He was the son of Raul.[264] Thus, he could be said to have a background providing him influence with God. He was also a member of the family. Because of the marriage covenant between his sister, Zipporah and Moses (Exodus 2:21), he was "blood" kin to Moses being his brother-in-law.[265] He also had experience of that foreboding barrier confronting

263 Numbers 10:29, "Hobab" [a]*chobaab*, **love**.

264 Numbers 10:29. "the son of Raguel", *ben-rauweel*, ***son of*** friend of God [*re'uw* = *ray'ah* = ***an associate of...*** *el* = ***the Almighty***] otherwise known as Jethro [Exodus 3:1; 4:18; 10:1-12 *Yithiro* = his excellency, from *yeh'ther* = in excess]...

265 Numbers 10:29, "the Midianite, Moses' father in law"...*ha-Midyaaniy*, ***the native who was under...****choteen* = ***contract***, he had contracted affinity to Moses through marriage, the word *ha-Midyaaniy* for "father in law" means ***[to the] one who circumcises***: it was the father of the bride's responsibility to circumcise his son in law to signify the new deal, the new prospects associated with the marriage covenant. As the result of this family covenant, he was a "covenant blood brother" to Moses and therefore under obligation to help the cause.

Moses and the children of Israel; the desert was his home.[266] He knew the roads, the trails, the oases, the lizards, the snakes, the scorpions and the way through. His knowledge would be invaluable to the tenderfoot Israelis who had only experienced the relative comforts of the domestic life, howbeit in slavery, of the Nile delta and river valley, the bread basket of the Mediterranean. They were naïve to the dangers of the desert. Death is a rude awakening even to those who are conditioned to stress. As we face unknown boundaries, we need to view them with the eyes of one experienced in that territory, not with our own naïve eyes.[267]

The Bargain, Numbers 10:29-32. The wording of Numbers 10:29-32 implies that Moses approached Hobab with some level of desperation (trepidation), showing how important it was to secure the best guide possible for their journey. The imperfect verb tenses that Moses used indicate a continued dialogue with Hobab that escalated in tension as it developed.[268] Moses, in his offer to attract Hobab to guide them, did not offer up-front payment, but he did offer a twofold compensation in

---

266 Numbers 10:31, "thou knowest how we are to encamp in the wilderness" *yaada^{a}taa,* Qal [active] perfect of *yawdah* = ***[who is] well acquainted with,*** having much savvy in, being familiar with...*chanoteenuw* = Qal infinitive: as to ***how to pitch a tent,*** where to camp, where to be at sundown...*b^{a}midbaar* = ***in the open, uninhabited desert...***

267 Numbers 10:31, "and thou mayest be to us instead of eyes." *w^{a}haayiytaa,* Wah conjunctive, Qal perfect of *hawyaw* = ***in conjunction [with finding spots to camp], you will exist...****laanuw,* ***for purpose of...****l^{a}eeynaayım,* as eyes, ***acting as a scout.***

268 Numbers10:29, "and Moses said", *w^{a}o'mer,* Wah consecutive, Qal [active] imperfect of *aw'mar* = ***in conjunction with their preparation to leave Mount Horeb,*** Moses *Mosheh* = ***the rescuer continually and persistently pleaded with Hobab...*** "come thou with us", *a^{a}kaah,* Qal [active] imperfect of *yawlak* = ***we are in the process of journeying...***[from *naw'lak* = to walk]; vs. 31, "and he said, leave us not I pray thee" *wayo'mer,* Wah consecutive, Qal [active] imperfect of *aw'mar,* [***in response to Hobab's refusal,*** Numbers 10:30], ***Moses*** put on the full court press, appealing to Hobab's emotions by putting him on a guilt trip, ***continued with increasing intensity to say...*** "leave us not I pray thee" *alnaa' ta^{a}zob,* Qal imperfect of *awzab'* = ***not now, not ever, begin to desert us, walk out on us, leave us in a lurch...***

terms of a commission to be paid upon arrival[269] and the opportunity to participate in a great event that would (likely) result in fame and fortune.[270] Moses told Hobab that he would have to trust him on this, or if he could not trust Moses, then trust the Lord (surely, He is trustworthy).[271] Making a good bargain concerning our mortality problem is important in terms of giving us the opportunity to address life with confidence. Bargains concerning my livelihood when I was growing up, were often conducted at cattle auction barns. One day in the 1950s when Daddy took me to the Abilene Livestock Auction, I happened to see an older couple in line to unload their Hereford bull. I always enjoyed my trips to the auction. Daddy would take me only when it rained (rare but usually euphoric events) thereby temporarily freeing me from the chores tying me to the farm. The auction was an exotic place with a boardwalk high above the wooden pens where cattle waited (patiently?) to be auctioned, an auction barn protecting the process from the weather and providing a café serving chicken fried steaks that smelled faintly of cow dung, and an auction ring with a lot of professional looking cattlemen sitting around it acting like they knew more about cattle than I would ever know. These men usually had unlit cigars in their mouths, wore pin-striped western shirts and Silverbelly Stetson hats. These "cattle traders" had a certain

---

269 Numbers 10:32, "it shall be, if thou go with us, it shall be",*w^{a}aayaah...w^{a}haayah,* Wah conjunctives, Qal [active] perfects of *hawyaw'* = ***you will truly come into your own***: as the pleading and level of desperation increased, Moses became redundant [pushy?] in his appeal to Hobab...

270 Numbers 10:29, "we are journeying into the place where the Lord said" *noc^{a}iym,* Qal participle active of *nawsah'* = ***we are in the process of pulling up tent pegs, packing up...****'el-,* ***in motion towards...****h^{a}maaowm,* ***the spot...****^{a}sher,* ***where...*** *'aamer,* ***we were challenged by YHWH, the self-existant one...*** "I will give it you" *'otaw,* ***the personal self...****'eteen,* Qal [active] imperfect of *nawthan,* ***I have begun to appoint...****laakem,* ***toward you...***

271 Numbers 10:29, "and we will do thee good" *w^{a}heeTanuw,* wah consecutive, Hiphil [causative] perfect of *yawTab',* ***we will make it right;*** Numbers 10:32, "it shall be that what goodness the Lord shall do to us, he will do to you" *haTowb,* ***the prosperity...****hahuw,* ***he himself...****^{a}sher,* ***in order that...****yeeyTiyb,* Hiphil [causative] imperfect of *yawtab'* = ***he will do the right thing...****YHWH,* ***the I AM...****imaanuw...****with us...****w^{a}heeTabnuw,* Wah conjunctive, Hiphil [causative] imperfect of *yawtab* = ***it will also be good...****laak,* ***toward you...***

conspiratorial look about them that implied they belonged to a private club whose purpose was to make money from deals at the expense of the uninitiated. They spoke a language no one else knew; (they even acted like they understood the rhythmic drumming of the auctioneer); and they had the look that indicated everyone else was there to learn from them and, in the meantime, contribute to their bank accounts. Because of this intimidating atmosphere, some country farmers, such as the ones I saw waiting to unload the bull, thought they might get a better deal by making a private arrangement with "brokers" who would befriend them and make an offer to buy their cattle before they unloaded them. As I watched the elderly couple bargain with one of these brokers, the bull seemingly tired of waiting for the trade to be consummated, leaned to his left, tilting the flimsy wooden trailer up on one wheel so that he gingerly stepped out of the trailer, wandering off toward another trailer full of young heifers. The couple continued their bargaining not realizing they had nothing to sell. Making a good trade has always been a source of confidence; a poor trade undermines any germ of confidence that may exist.

Rejection, Numbers 10:30-31. Moses wanted Hobab to be all that he could have been and therefore spent considerable effort pleading him to live up to his name, reputation and covenant promise. But, Hobab's name could be taken in two ways. The meaning of loving comes with a barb because the root of the word differentiates a particular kind of love through the picture of the love of a mother in sheltering her child or the love of the child in response to the mother's protection, especially the protection of the womb.[272] Thus, the fear was that Hobab might, when push came to shove, run and hide, seeking protection from the unknown. He might not be so trustworthy as to stick to the task through thick and thin. In this regard, he might typify humanity as being basically unreliable. He was ultimately true to this aspect of his name. He flat

272 Numbers 10:29, "Hobab" *l*[a]*chbaab,* to cherish [from *khawbab* = ***to hide*** {as in the bosom, related to *hob* = bosom}]...

rejected Moses' offer of fame and fortune.[273] Hobab was homesick and chose to be domestic instead of adventurous. Who can blame him for putting his family first? But on the other hand, he failed to live up to his covenant promise to his in-laws. And he failed to be an instrumental part of the most consequential journey of mankind, the journey that pictures the great journey required of each of us, the journey through the desert-like portal of death beyond the Edge. Moses needed a scout whose fundamental motive was true love because this motive would assure that when the "chips were down" he would not "cut and run". Hobab failed to live up to this standard. Fortunately, Jesus, the true servant of the Covenant epitomizes true love and, therefore, merits our blind trusts as a guide across the deserted barrier of death. Abandonment is possibly the greatest fear (autophobia) that one can have in life. When the tide is running in your favor, many seem to want on board, but when the tide runs against you, it is much harder to find colleagues. The effects are much worse when the leader, the scout, abandons the effort. In that case, the situation becomes like the proverbial "rats abandoning the sinking ship". The tide may run against you many times in your life. It is during these times that your colleagues can show their true colors. In my experience, when the tide turned and the organization I worked for seemed to abandon its mission of performing research useful to agricultural producers, only one of my colleagues proved to have the love for the organization and the self-sacrificing boldness required to make a stand. Dr. Charles Long, longtime administrator, scientist, educator, agriculturalist, and cow dog breeder stood against the flow. Charles' tenacity in going against the flow can be observed in the scars he carries. He carries a scar near his mouth where a bull kicked him, breaking his jaw. He endured six weeks of having his mouth wired shut to facilitate healing of the jaw. He walks stiffly, like all worn-out cowboys do because

273 Numbers 10:30, "and he said unto him" *wayo'mer,* Wah consecutive, Qal [active] imperfect of *awmar',* ***[Hobab's] continuing answer was...*** "but I will depart" *im-kiy,* ***my alternative is...****'artsiy,* ***my soil...****w^{a}el,* ***in conjunction toward...****mowlabtiy* ***my family,*** emphatic...*'eelek,* Qal [active] imperfect of *hawlak',* ***I will begin my journey [home].***

of the scar he carries from the time a horse bucked him off. Before his rude collision with the ground, he landed on the saddle horn, breaking his pelvis in two. He rides horses to this day, rounding up cattle and hunting for feral hogs in the east Texas underbrush. Charles has proven to have the qualities found lacking in Hobab and in most people when the chips are down. But, the ultimate turn of the tide we all face is death. This crisis requires a scout with credentials not found in any person to have ever lived except Jesus. The true scout will never abandon you, even as you go beyond the Edge.

Rethink Possible,[274] Numbers 10:33-34, John 14:4-6

"Crown Him the Lord of life, who triumphed over the grave,
And rose victorious in the strife for those He came to save.
His glories now we sing, Who died, and rose on high,
Who died eternal life to bring, and lives that death may die."

> *Crown Him with Many Crowns*, circa 1866, words by Godfrey Thring, music by George J. Elvey.

Illustration 6, Death Valley Days. As the children of Israel learned, the desert is a good place to die: a head stone in the Gobi Desert of western China (left); a windmill in south Texas where buzzards wait for food (right).

274 "Rethink possible. Expand your boundaries of Can. See whats on the other side of Too Far. Play the Angels Advocate. Outsmart Can't. Put a restriction on your limit." 2012. AT&T slogan. www.att.com.

Death Valley Days,[275] **Numbers 10:33-34.** So, literally with a cloud hanging over their heads,[276] Moses and the children of Israel gave up civilization as they knew it to begin their fateful journey across the unknown passage of entry into the Promised Land.[277] Giving up their argument with Hobab that was obviously going nowhere, they departed from the mount of God without an experienced guide.[278] The significance of the mention of the three-day journey[279] is unclear. But, comparison to Jesus' three-day "journey" in the grave seems intuitively plausible in the light of the peculiar replacement for the absent Hobab as scout for the expedition. The replacement guide was the Ark of the Covenant, the recognized prescient symbol for the Messiah. The Ark is recognized as being a foreordination of the Messiah, the pioneer of death, because of several of its characteristics. The Hebrew word for Ark is translated in other places as "coffin" or "sarcophagus".[280] It had the dimensions of a sarcophagus, symbolic of death.[281] It was a box constructed of a wood whose name meant to pierce.[282] It was a peculiar coffin, because it contained, not a dead body, but the basics of the covenant/law which proved to be too high a standard for man and, therefore, the instrument of condemnation

---

275 *Death Valley Days*, 1930, Radio and Television series created by Ruth Woodman.

276 Numbers 10:34, "And the cloud of the LORD was upon them by day, when they went out of the camp."

277 Numbers 10:33, "and they departed from" *wayicuw*, Wah consecutive, Qal [active] imperfect of *nawsah'*, ***in consequence to Hobab's rejection, the children of Israel continued to pull up their tent pegs to start their journey from...***

278 Numbers10:33, "the mount of the Lord" *meeher YHWH*, ***the mount of I AM...***

279 Numbers 10:33, "three days journey" *derek shaloshet yaamiy*, ***on the road got three days...***

280 Numbers 10:33, "the ark of the covenant of the LORD" *wa'aarown*, Wah conjunctive of *awraw'*, in conjunction with the gathering of sticks in order to make a coffin, sarcophagus.

281 Exodus 25:10 "two cubits and a half shall be the length thereof, and a cubit and a half the breadth thereof, and a cubit and a half the height thereof"

282 Exodus 25:10 "And they shall make an ark of shittim wood", *shiTiym*, acacia [from *shotet* = to pierce].

and thus of death.[283] It was covered with a "mercy seat" upon which the blood of sacrifice was to be sprinkled, symbolic of atonement and the salvation to be brought by the sacrifice of the Messiah.[284] The question of how the Messiah provides salvation from our Covenant with Death is answered by the symbolic use of the Ark as a guide for crossing the desert, a good place to die and, therefore, emblematic of the valley of death. Moses, if not the children of Israel, trusted the Ark of the Covenant to lead them across the desert. In like manner, we must trust the servant of the covenant, the Messiah, for guidance across the foreboding desert of death.

Over Which Hilltop,[285] **John 14:4-5.** Speaking of guides, after the allusion to Numbers 10, Jesus continued His discussion with His disciples on the eve of His death concerning their impending journey. He completed His *remez* with a question/answer exchange with one of His disciples, Thomas. Jesus precipitated this exchange by showing the disciples they needed Him to guide them. He told them something that was not intuitively obvious to them but was the basis for their need for the Rock to save them from their Covenant with Death. He told them that they knew where He was going, that they knew the rendezvous point where they could meet again.[286] He also indicated to them their need for a guide, implicitly Him as their guide by telling them that they knew how to get to the camping spot, at

283 Romans 6:23 "For the wages of sin is death; but the gift of God is eternal life through Jesus Christ our Lord."

284 Exodus 25:17 "a mercy seat" *kaparet* = lid [from *kawfar'* = to cover over, placate, cancel, pardon, make propitiation, **make atonement for**].

285 "I've got a mansion just over the hilltop, In that bright land where we'll never grow old; And someday yonder we will never more wander, But walk the streets that are purest gold." *Mansion Over the Hilltop*, 1949, written by Ira Stanphill, sung notably by Elvis Presley, album *His Hand in Mine*.

286 John 14:4, "and whither I go ye know" *kai hupou*, ***and my destination that...*** *ego hupage*, present indicative: ***I now lead you under...****oidate*, ***you continue to perceive intuitively, but have never experienced...***

least they had been there in their minds.[287] Since we are on the same journey as the disciples, in need of a postmortem rendezvous with the trail blazer, we can identify with Thomas in his anxious questioning of Jesus about the details of the journey. I once worked with a south Texas cattleman, Bill Soyars, who had voluminous knowledge about cows and how to work them. He would often give directions as to how the cowboys (including me) could accomplish a roundup. It usually involved, at daybreak, riding out a large, brushy pasture in some systematic way, with the cowboys acting in concert to herd all the cattle toward some rendezvous point, usually a windmill with a set of cow pens. It was usually only after the process had begun, when I was alone, getting to know the brush, the dust, and the rattlesnakes intimately, that I would become aware that I didn't understand his directions (e.g. usually it was something like there turned out to be more than one windmill; which one did he mean?). Only then did I realize that it would have been better to have asked questions up front concerning the vagaries of the process. The only reason I hadn't asked these questions early on was that I did not want to reveal my ignorance. So, we owe a debt of gratitude to Thomas for his timely questions to Jesus to the effect that we don't have a clue how to travel in that desert.[288] We must admit that, without an experienced guide to lead us into this unknown passage, we are lost.

The Trail Blazer, John 14:6. Fortunately for us, Thomas expressed this despair of feeling lost in his question so that Jesus could answer in

287 John 14:4, "and the way ye know" *teen hoden*, ***and you perceive the road required to get you there...***

288 John 14:5, "Thomas saith unto him" *Legei*, present indicative of *lego*, ***now alleges...*** *auto*, **to him...** *Thoomas*, ***the twin***, [Hebrew: *tawome* = a duplicate]..."
"Lord, we know not whither thou goest" *Kurie*, ***supreme author...****ouk oidamen*, present indicative of *eido* = ***we have absolutely no idea...****pou*, ***to what spot...*** *hupageis*, present indicative of *hupago*, ***you now depart to,...*** "and how can we know the way" *Poos*, ***by what means...****dunametha*, present indicative middle of *dunamai*, ***do we have capacity...****teen hodon*, ***as to the spot...****eidenai*, present infinitive of *eido* = ***to instinctively, intuitively perceive...****teen hodon*, the road, ***the journey***.

terms of how we can attain such a guide. He answered by saying that if we have confidence in Him as the guide in our journey through this life, we can be assured that we can have confidence in Him to lead us in that journey/road on the other side of the grave ("I am the way"). Through this confidence in Him as guide, we have the reason for the journey, that we might attain full revelation without distortion ("I am... the truth"). Through this confidence in Him as guide, we can also have the vitality and motivation to make the whole journey on both sides of the grave ("I am...the life").[289] No other possible guide has experienced the total journey on both sides of the grave, is willing and able to give us the unadulterated truth about the journey, and can provide us the vision (motivation), vigor and stamina to make the journey home to the Father.

289 John14:6, "Jesus saith unto him," *Legei auto ho Ieesous*, present indicative of *lego*: ***The Jesus now says to him...*** "I am the way" *Ego eimi*, present indicative: ***I, even I*** [emphatic] ***continue to exist as...****hee hodon*, ***the*** journey, ***road...*** "the truth" *hee alleetheia*, ***the full revelation,*** with no secrets, nothing hidden, nothing held back, ***illuminating the road...*** "and the life" *kai hee zooee*, ***and the vitality,*** quickness, vigor... "no man cometh unto the Father but by me" *oudeis*, ***no one, not even one...****erchomai*, present indicative middle: ***makes progress toward...****ton Patera*, ***the progenitor...****ei meh*, ***except...****di emou*, ***through the channel of me.***

EPILOGUE

We know intuitively that we are more than the sum of our physical parts. We have an identity beyond that explained by the totality of proteins coded in our DNA. We have something that is innate that characterizes each of us. We call this identity our personality. The Hebrews called it *nephesh* or *ruwach;* the Greeks called it *pnuma* or *pseuche.* We know we were born with it. We know we will die with it. We know that each of us is distinctive in it, each of us having a different flavor. Our personality expresses itself in what the old television show *The Twilight Zone*[290] called the fifth dimension, the imagination. It is not a stretch to believe that this essential element of our being outlasts our time on this earth. It is also within reason that this "essence" is on an epic journey. This is not hard to comprehend because the journey concept is endemic in the very fabric of humanity. This is revealed in nearly all of our literature in that all major protagonists (e.g. *Odysseus, Beowulf, Macbeth, Don Quixote, Harry Potter, etc.*) in our literature are depicted to be on epic journeys. All journeymen require experienced leadership in order to be successful. This success requires that the journeyman has confidence in the competence and skill of a qualified guide. This confidence provides the journeyman stability even in unfamiliar territory. This confidence frees us, as journeymen, from the illusions that hold us back. The biggest

290 *The Twilight Zone*, 1959-1964, 1985-1989, television anthology created by Rod Serling.

illusion that governs our lives is that our journey ends in failure (in death). Confidence in this illusion forces us to make a private deal with ourselves (our Covenant with Death) amounting to creative methods to escape the specter of death. Confidence in this illusion (in contrast to confidence in the Qualified Guide) amounts to living a lie. Living the lie burdens us with guilt, fear, and doubt (the various currencies of the death tax resulting from our Covenant with Death) to the extent that we cannot freely progress on our journey. We are freed from the burden of the death tax by confidence in the only qualified guide that won't abandon us at the great journey transition point of death. That guide is Jesus, the Cornerstone. Dependence upon Him frees us to live the pioneering life beyond the Edge.

8813952R00093

Made in the USA
San Bernardino, CA
22 February 2014